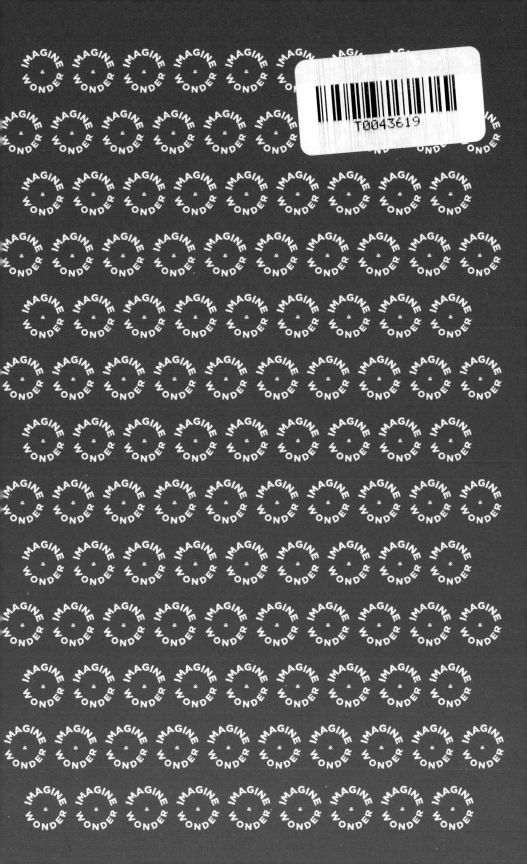

This book can be toke-
nized. Scan the code to
claim the digital token.

TICKET TO RIDE

*Legendary Beatle Locations
For The Day Tripper*

Dr. Angie McCartney

Foreword by Freda Kelly

This is a smart book which means whenever you see a QR code you can scan it with your smart phone and visit the linked content. For example, scan the code below to visit www.imagineandwonder.com

PRINTED WITH
SOY INK

Trademark of American Soybean Association

MIX
Paper from
responsible sources
FSC® C017606

ISBN: 9781637610114 (Hardback)
Library of Congress Control Number: 2021943904
1st Edition
This book, story, and any associated content is protected. © Copyright 2022 by Dr. Angie McCartney.
Published by Imagine and Wonder Publishers, New York. 28 Sycamore Lane, Irvington New York, NY10533
United States of America. Telephone: 646.644.0403
Printed in China by Hung Hing Off-set Printing Co. Ltd.

DEDICATION

To Ruth, my beacon, my inspiration, my motivation, and countless other "...ations," (including libations), and to Martin, my creative guide and mentor. (Herr Direktor to his friends.)

For their tenacity, endless love, patience and persuasion, encouragement and guidance.

Without whom ...

What more can I say? With my gratitude and love.

From Angie "The Asset" aka "Green Bin"

QR CODE INSTRUCTIONS

HOW TO SCAN: OPEN, AIM + TAP

Open the camera on your phone   **Aim it at the flowcode**   **Tap the banner that appears**

This book contains "scan-able" codes which will magically transport you on your smart phone or tablet to McCartney.com web pages containing precise map links, images, in some cases videos and a full colour, digital "experience."

You can either (a) download a free QR reader from the App Store or Google Play, OR (b) simply open your smart-phone camera, hold it over the code and tap the link to flowto.it that pops up…just more ways to enjoy the long and winding road of Fab Four locations in this book!

TABLE OF CONTENTS

		Page #
Foreword by Freda Kelly		2
There Are Places I Remember		3
Tune In, Turn On		4
Hamburg	10 Locations	5
Liverpool	49 Locations	23
London	12 Locations	114
Los Angeles	7 Locations	139
New York	8 Locations	156

FOREWORD

By BEATLES' FAN CLUB SECRETARY AND BRIAN EPSTEIN'S ASSISTANT, Freda Kelly

I have known Angie for a long time. We met during the 60's when she married Paul McCartney's Dad, who I called Uncle Jim.

Angie came into the Fan Club office quite regularly. She was most welcome, because she brought biscuits! Over the years, we have kept in touch and also met up a number of times.

Having known her for many decades, and also knowing her knack of both organised thinking and storytelling, I am sure you will find the stories and QR codes in this book both interesting and funny.

Travel safely, and please make sure you put Liverpool at the top of your list!

Freda Kelly
Liverpool, UK, 2020

Freda and Angie in Beverly Hills, CA at Julien's Auctions
at the event featuring one of Ringo's original drum kit sales.
Photo: Ruth McCartney

THERE ARE PLACES
I REMEMBER

Playa del Rey, CA

This book was written during the 2020 COVID-19 lockdown, as more and more of my social media family told me that they were dreaming of travelling again.

Since I am constantly asked by friends who are Beatle fans (would I have any *OTHER* kind of friends?), to put together tour itineraries for their trips to Fab Four destinations, I finally decided that there was no better time to research and publish the ultimate destinations guide to Liverpool, London, Hamburg, New York and Los Angeles.

I've also pulled rank and availed myself of our in-house, McCartney Multimedia concept of using QR Codes to link you to maps, images, in some cases videos, and bridge the gap between the printed page and your smart-phone.

Travel safely, and when in Liverpool, have a nice cuppa tea for me!

Cheers!
Angie

TUNE IN, TURN ON

If you'd like to tune in to Liverpool radio before you go there to bone up on our Scouse accent, scan the code below with your smart phone to tune in to Liverpool Legends like Pete Price, Billy Butler and the whole crew on the newly launched **LiverpoolLive247.co.uk** using the Radio.garden App.

All photos are free and commercially available to use as provided by Wikimedia Commons licensing.

SECTION 1: HAMBURG, GERMANY

Welcome to Hamburg - Willkommen!

From their humble beginnings in Liverpool, the Beatles' first step towards a real career was when their first Booking Agent / Manager Allan Williams decided to take them to Hamburg. They were very excited at the prospect of going abroad together.

Their first trip was in Allan's beat-up old van, and that was an adventure in itself. First of all, getting them ready for a trip to this cold and wet area of Germany, packing all of them into the vehicle, plus instruments and luggage, and their various picnics for the journey.

When they arrived, cold, hungry and tired, they were shunted off to their first venue, and found that they would be sleeping in the Bambi Kino, behind the screen, on beds that, were to say the least, lumpy and uncomfortable. But by this time, they were so exhausted they would have happily slept on the floor.

And so it began. Their crippling schedule, day and night, playing to a usually drunk and abusive crowd. Their lives were saved (to a degree), when the lady cloakroom attendant started stealing food for them and giving them Preludin tablets ("prellies") to help them get through the long nights.

But Hamburg was where they really began to realize what a career was going to mean. They bonded together, in true Liverpool style, shored up by their sense of humour, which was a Godsend, and began to mold themselves into the professionals that would eventually catch the attention of Brian Epstein, who took them to the "toppermost of the poppermost" to quote one of John Lennon's catch phrases.

They learned to cope, learned to survive, if not for Hamburg, then the rest of their history may never have happened.

I remember Jim telling me that, the first time he opened the front door to greet Paul on his return to 20 Forthlin Road, for a split second, he didn't recognize him, he looked so pale and thin, undernourished, and exhausted. I can only imagine the TLC Paul came in for from his Dad until he was back on his feet again.

Scan this code with your smart-phone camera or QR Reader app to view the year-round weather in Hamburg and more information.

Akustik Studio

Kirchenallee 57, Hamburg, Germany

S-Bahn - Hamburg Hauptbahnhof

Now the site of NAGEL German Restaurants where you can enjoy a coffee or a "bier" at the spot where the early Beatles recorded in Germany.

Whilst early Beatles' manager Allan Williams was in Hamburg, he arranged for a private recording session for his new band at Akustik Studio, owned by a Mr. Breul, located in an office building in the city centre.

As lead singer, Williams had chosen Lu Walters, the bass player with Rory Storm and The Hurricanes, and to back him, he arranged for John Lennon, Paul McCartney, Ringo Starr, (who was still in Rory Storm's Hurricanes at the time). It is not confirmed whether the lead guitarist on the session was either George Harrison or Ty Brien, also of The Hurricanes.

The session happened on a Saturday afternoon, October 15th 1960. It has not been made clear what the song title was, or what the outcome of that session was either.

Scan this code with your smart-phone camera or QR Reader app to view the map, directions and more information.

Bambi Kino
Paul-Roosen Strasse 33, Hamburg 22727, Germany

It opened in 1959 originally named as the Luna Kino. In the early-1960's, the Bambi Kino was just a little run-down cinema. The Beatles camped out in a storage room behind the screen on their first visit to Hamburg in August-November 1960 to play their stint at The Indra Club. The Bambi Kino was owned by Bruno Koschmider, who also owned the Indra Club and the Kaiserkeller in the basement of Grosse Freiheit 36, both of which were where The Beatles performed during that initial visit to the city.

When Pete Best and Paul went back to the Bambi Kino to collect their luggage before going home, the place was in darkness. They found a condom in their luggage, stuck it to a nail on the wall, set fire to it to get some light to find their stuff. There was no real damage done, but Koschmider reported them both for attempted arson and they spent 3 hours in the local Police Station.

A scary experience, I'm sure.

The Bambi Kino closed down shortly after and was converted into apartments. As a nod to its former fame, someone has painted a "Bambi" fawn on the garage door.

Scan this code with your smart-phone camera or QR Reader app to view the map, directions and more information.

_____

Beatles-Platz
Reeperbahn 174, 20359 Hamburg, Germany
Tel: +49 630 949 950

The Platz was built to commemorate Hamburg's place in Fab Four History. The original design was submitted by Dose und Stitch architects during a common open round of proposals. The whole project wound up costing approximately half a million Euros and was jointly funded by donors, fans, sponsors and the City.

This Beatles memorial consists of metal statues of the band members as well as song names of successful songs. The initial engravings held some spelling mistakes such as *Drive **ME** car, Sgt. **PEPPERS** Lonely Hearts Club Band* and ***CANT** Buy Me Love*, without their apostrophes, which couldn't be corrected before the unveiling on September 11th, 2008.

By now, the incorrect plates have been exchanged and all is right with the world.

Scan this code with your smart-phone camera or QR Reader app to view the map, directions and more information.

Ernst-Merck-Halle

St. Petersburger Str. 30, 20355 Hamburg, Germany

This was a 5,600 capacity indoor arena located in Hamburg, opened in 1950. It was named after a prominent German businessman and Politician

Ernst Merck. It hosted concerts until June 1986 when it was closed and demolished. The Hamburg Messe complex now stands in its place.

A number of well-known artists appeared there including, of course, The Beatles, who played there on 26th June 1966, after a three-year absence from the city. Scan the code to watch the video.

They played 2 sets, each of which was seen by 5,600 people. They didn't get a break between the shows as they had to attend a press conference. Dozens of people were arrested for rioting during the shows, both inside and outside the venue.

Also appearing here over the years were The Rolling Stones, Kiss, Iron Maiden, Queen, Pink Floyd, The Who, Santana and Deep Purple.

Scan this code with your smart-phone camera or QR Reader app to view the map, directions and more information.

Friedrich Ebert Halle
Alter Postweg 34, 21075 Hamburg, Germany
S-Bahn Heimfeld:

The Beatles recorded an instrumental titled "Cry For A Shadow" on 22nd June 1961 at The Friedrich Ebert Halle Studios in Hamburg. They were there as a back-up band to singer Tony Sheridan.

George composed the song, together with John, and it was in the style of the other famous Group, The Shadows. At that time, The Shadows, with their distinctive style, had made a name for themselves as Cliff Richard's Band and they were hugely successful.

This song is the only Beatles title that credits Harrison and Lennon as writers.

It was intended to be released as the B-side of "Why", another Tony Sheridan song with The Beatles, but the record company chose to release another song instead. In early 1964, as The Beatles were gaining popularity, the record company Polydor decided to release it, with "Why" changed to the B side.

According to Bill Harry, editor of the Mersey Beat newspaper, *"Cry for a Shadow's"* original title was *"Beatle Bop"*. It was also released in 1995 as part of the Anthology 1 compilation.

Scan this code with your smart-phone camera or QR Reader app to view the map, directions and more information.

The Indra Club

Grosse Freiheit 64, Hamburg, 22767, Germany

The original Beatles (including Stuart Sutcliffe and Pete Best) played here many times between August 1960 and December 1962. The Beatles' first Booking Agent/Manager, Allan Williams, got them their first gigs, having previously had success with another one of his Acts, Derry & The Seniors.

They took on Pete Best as their regular drummer just a few days before they were to set off to Germany for the beginning of their big adventure.

It was there that they met Astrid Kirchherr, who was to figure largely in their lives and careers.

She was the originator of their famous "Beatles" haircuts, which took the world by storm. Thus began their new image, to be followed by tailored suits, Beatle boots et al, when Brian Epstein entered their lives and decided that their image was all important.

It was during their time in Hamburg that Astrid and Stuart Sutcliffe came together. Stuart decided to leave the band and concentrate on his studies. He then lived with Astrid.

Scan this code with your smart-phone camera or QR Reader app to view the map, directions and more information.

Kaiserkeller
Underneath Große Freiheit 36, 20359 Hamburg, Germany

Kaiserkeller is a music club in the St. Pauli quarter of Hamburg, Germany, near the red-light district called The Reeperbahn. It was opened by impresario Bruno Koschmider on October 14th, 1959. The Beatles had a contract with Kaiserkeller to begin to play there in 1960, a full 4 years before their USA Ed Sullivan debut.

They played for 7 or 8 hours a night, SEVEN NIGHTS A WEEK. This was their second club gig in Hamburg, the first being at Koschmider's Indra Club. The flimsy and dangerous stage of the Kaiserkeller was made of planks of wood balanced on the top of beer crates. One onlooker and fan, was a local German boy by the name of Klaus Voormann, who would go on to be instrumental in shaping the Beatles' lives by introducing them to his friend Astrid Kirchherr who gave them their famous "Mop Top" haircuts, and later Klaus would go on to be the artist who drew the pen and ink cover for the LP "Revolver".

Today the Kaiserkeller is an alternative Rock Club in the basement that belongs to the "Große Freiheit 36" club, which is above it on street level.

Scan this code with your smart-phone camera or QR Reader app to view the map, directions and more information.

The Hard Rock Cafe

Brucke 5, Bei Den St. Pauli Landungsbrücken, Bei den St. Pauli, 20359 Hamburg

Tel: +49 40 300 68480

As with all Hard Rock Cafés around the world, this one specialises in rock 'n roll memorabilia, always a draw for the tourists, cameras at the ready. Coupled with a great menu, and great German beer, who could ask for anything more? And of course, yes, they have their fair share of Beatles memorabilia here.

Oh, but wait, they also have a great 17 page catalogue of the goodies that you can either purchase when visiting, or online, with lots of convenient ways to pay for your order. They only deliver by mail within the Hamburg area though. However, there are now so many Hard Rock Cafés worldwide, that wherever you live, you can probably order online and have your order delivered to the address of your choice.

Please do remember to carry your ID if you're ordering a "Bier"...in fact, this is important wherever you are travelling, including Germany!

Scan this code with your smart-phone camera or QR Reader app to view the map, directions and more information.

The Star-Club, Hamburg

Grosse Freiheit 39, St. Pauli, Hamburg, Germany

The famous Star-Club in Hamburg was one of several owned by Horst Fascher and a partner. This particular club opened on Friday 13th April 1962, and closed on 31st December 1969. The building was subsequently burned to the ground in 1987.

It first really rose to prominence in April 1962, when The Beatles began playing there. They played at several venues owned by Horst Fascher, who was a tough taskmaster and made them play long hours with little rest in between.

The stories of their adventures over this time are legend. They were taken there by their first Booking Agent/Manager, Allan Williams and when they returned home, Paul's father barely recognized his own son when he rang the front door bell. He was so pale and thin, from lack of sleep, too many "uppers" to keep them awake through the long hours, and not enough nourishment.

By the way, Grosse Freiheit is a side street of the Reeperbahn, the red light district of Hamburg. So watch your purses and wallets!

Scan this code with your smart-phone camera or QR Reader app to view the map, directions and more information.

The Top Ten Club
Reeperbahn 136 , Hamburg, 20359 Germany

The Top Ten Club was a music club in Hamburg's St. Pauli district at Reeperbahn 136, which opened on 31 October 1960 and kept its name until 1994.

The Beatles appeared at the Top Ten Club with crooner Tony Sheridan from April 1st to July 1st 1961 for a total of 92 nights performing continuously in the Top Ten Club.

They played seven hours a night, eight hours on weekends. There was a fifteen-minute pause after each hour. Each member of The Beatles was to be paid 35 deutschmarks per day - which, in those days was the equivalent of $4 US.

Since 2008 the venue has been called *MOONDOO*, and the current operator is listed as "Lago Bay Betriebsgesellschaft GmbH".

Ticket to Ride

In 1994, the *London Club Dome*, in Tufnell Park in the London Borough of Islington district, was transformed into the Top Ten Club for the Stuart Sutcliffe-centric film Backbeat.

Scan this code with your smart-phone camera or QR Reader app to view the map, directions and more information.

SECTION 2 : LIVERPOOL

Background Image / Green Screen Photo Credit:
TheGuideLiverpool.com – thanks to Jay Hynd!

Get The Kettle (and Yer Wellies) On!

Liverpool has a fascinating history. Amongst my own earliest recollections are being on my Dad's shoulders, watching King George and Queen Mary at the opening of the first Mersey Tunnel. (Yes, I'm THAT old).

The Liverpool we know today is vastly different from the days when the Beatles were wartime babies, born when the nightly air raids were devastating and flattening the City. Their world was black and white, and then it gradually changed to Technicolor, and psychedelic hues when the hippy times came along, and their path covered many miles and hues.

Ticket to Ride

The Beatles' story began when John Lennon decided to get a group together, The Quarrymen, during his days at Quarry Bank School with some of his schoolmates. They were a fairly ragged combo in the beginning, and as John was to say later, that all changed the day that Ivan Vaughan brought along his friend, Paul McCartney to St. Peter's Garden Fete in Woolton.

John and Paul immediately hit it off, although Paul was a little perturbed to find that John's breath smelled of beer. That'll show you how innocent he was in those days.

But by degrees, he fitted himself into the group, followed by his young friend, George Harrison, and so began their journey to stardom. They were always convinced they would make it one day, but to what extent, they had no vision. As I write this in the year 2020, the fame of The Beatles is still growing, and not showing any sign of slowing down. Such is the appeal of their music, magic and mayhem. Long may they prosper.

Once Brian Epstein entered their lives after seeing them at The Cavern, along with Alistair Taylor, he guided them towards a more professional on stage presence, (which meant no ciggies, no beer bottles, and chatting up the girls in the audience). Then came the tailored collarless jackets, the first ones made by Beno Dorn in Birkenhead for £40 GBP (quid) per suit, then Dougie Millings in London, then the Beatles haircuts, Beatle boots, etc., starting an endless string of merchandise which still sells like hot cakes today.

And from Liverpool, they embarked on their many trips to Germany, and Hamburg was where they really shaped themselves into musicians.

Scan this code with your smart-phone camera or QR Reader app to view the map, directions and more information.

Admiral Grove

10 Admiral Grove, Dingle, Liverpool L8 8BH

A small property in The Dingle, Liverpool, this is the house in which Richard Starkey, now Sir Ringo Starr lived for twenty years during his childhood and formative years.

Starr's infant school, St. Silas Primary School, on Pengwern Street, was yards away from his front door. He was a sickly child and, due to his many absences from school, was taught to read and write at home. A severe bout of peritonitis led him to spend most of his seventh year at the Royal Children's Hospital.

When Starr was 13, his mother Elsie married a Londoner, Harry Graves.

The Starkeys' local pub, *The Empress*, where Elsie was a barmaid, adjoins Admiral Grove. The pub was immortalized in 1970 by being featured on the front cover of Starr's first solo album *Sentimental Journey*.

In 2016, the house was bought by Beatles fan Jackie Holmes for £70,000 - Jackie also owns houses owned previously by George Harrison and John Lennon's mother Julia.

PLEASE RESPECT THE OCCUPANTS AS THIS IS NOT A PUBLIC MUSEUM.

Scan this code with your smart-phone camera or QR Reader app to view the map, directions and more information.

12 Ardwick Road
aka Paul McCartney's Childhood Home
Speke, Liverpool L24 2UA

Ardwick Road in the Speke area of Liverpool was another of the many rental properties where the McCartney family lived, due to the fact that Paul and Michael's mother, Mary, was a midwife and was frequently housed in the district where she worked as a peripatetic midwife. (Yes, go on, look it up - it means mobile).

This was their home previous to moving to 20 Forthlin Road, before Paul was able to make his Dad independent by buying him his own home, Rembrandt, on the other side of the Mersey in Gayton, Wirral.

The Speke estate was built by Liverpool Corporation with a plan to build a new town for all classes of people. Unfortunately, this didn't work out as they had planned, it quickly became beset by crime, gangs and a place to avoid.

Although they didn't know one another yet, the Harrisons lived in the same area, and Paul and George would get to know one another later on, meeting up on the bus to school (The Liverpool Institute). And now, the site of the Liverpool John Lennon Airport is only a mile or two away…little did they think then what their futures would hold.

PLEASE RESPECT THE OCCUPANTS AS THIS IS NOT A PUBLIC MUSEUM.

Scan this code with your smart-phone camera or QR Reader app to view the map, directions and more information.

12 Arnold Grove
Wavertree, Liverpool L15 8HP, UK
Aka George Harrison's Birthplace and Childhood Home
The house is the birthplace and childhood home of George Harrison.

It is a small terraced house in a cul-de-sac where George's parents, Harold and Louise, moved to in 1931 following their marriage. The rent was ten shillings (aka ten bob) a week. All four of the couple's kids were born at home here with a midwife in attendance: Louise (16th August 1931), Harry (1934), Peter (20th July 1940) and George (25th February 1943).

George recalled that the only heating was a single coal fire, and the house was so cold in winter that he and his brothers dreaded getting up in the morning because it was freezing cold and they had to use the outside toilet. The house had tiny rooms – only ten feet by ten feet – and a small iron cooking stove in the back room, which was used as a kitchen. Describing the back garden, Harrison wrote it had "a one-foot wide flower bed, a toilet, a dustbin fitted to the back wall and a little hen house where we kept cockerels."

George lived here for the first six years of his life, by which time the family had been living there for nearly 20 years. They finally moved out to a new council estate in Speke, near the McCartney Family on 2nd January 1950.

Scan this code with your smart-phone camera or QR Reader app to view the map, directions and more information.

---

20 Forthlin Road

Aka Paul's childhood home, Liverpool 18, United Kingdom

This is the home where Paul McCartney lived with his Dad, my late husband Jim, and brother Michael, up until he became famous as a Beatle. He then moved to London, and bought his Dad a mock Tudor house on the Wirral Peninsula called Rembrandt, where he still stays when he is in the Liverpool area.

Forthlin is a small council house, which now belongs to the National Trust of Great Britain, due to its historic value. Many tours drive by, and tours of inside can be arranged in advance with any one of the many Liverpool tour operators.

An interesting little side note: After Jim, Paul and Michael had moved out, it's said that a copy of Rupert The Bear was found which bore the inscription:

This book belongs to Paul and Michael McCartney of 12 Ardwick Road, Speke. (Their previous home).

Scan this code with your smart-phone camera or QR Reader app to view the map, directions and more information, including the James Corden episode of Carpool Karaoke where he took Paul back to the house to play the piano.

---

3 Gambier Terrace
Hope Street Quarter, Liverpool L1 7BG

Gambier Terrace is a street of 19th century properties, close to the two Liverpool Cathedrals, where John Lennon and Stuart Sutcliffe lived, celebrating their freedom from the restrictions of family life.

Stuart moved in there first, then asked his neighbours if they would agree to let his homeless friend (John Lennon) to move in with him. They agreed.

John used to take Cynthia Powell, his future wife there for romantic trysts. It was sparsely furnished, with little comfort or convenience, but it was where they were able to hide away from prying eyes.

Numbers 1 through 10 are now considered luxury apartments, with a Grade II listing on the National Register, and its value has increased considerably since those days. In fact, in August 2019, a 3 bedroomed apartment was listed at GBP 280,000. That's the equivalent of almost $370,000 US! Quite an upgrade, I would say.

Scan this code with your smart-phone camera or QR Reader app to view the map, directions and more information.

---

4 Lads Who Shook The World Sculpture

15 Mathew Street, Liverpool (above the entrance to the former Eric's Club)

This is a sculpture by the late Arthur Dooley which stands on the wall outside of The Cavern.

It was the inspiration of Liverpool's own legendary broadcaster Pete Price.

In the early days of their accelerating fame, Pete made a suggestion to the City Council that a statue to our local heroes might be fitting, both as a tribute to them, and as a tourist attraction.

They were not in favour of the idea at the time but unbeknownst to him, news of this idea reached many of his fans, who began a campaign in the press, mainly The Liverpool Echo, supporting the idea, and after much discussion, it was agreed that the plan would go ahead, and Pete, who was by then the Master of Ceremonies at the now defunct Shakespeare Theatre, organized a fundraiser.

A gala star-studded evening fundraiser was duly put in place, with Frankie Vaughn headlining. Tom O'Connor and The Black Abbots were star performers. Originally, Frankie Vaughn didn't think he would be available, so he wasn't featured on the posters, but at the last minute, he was able to change his plans and joined in to auction Beatles memorabilia along with Pete Price, which resulted in raising more money than they had anticipated.

Jim and I attended, and later in the evening, bid on a painting for a sum I can't remember, and we went home in a taxi proudly sporting our new acquisition.

Pete got in touch with sculptor and artist Arthur Dooley and thus the project began. Arthur Dooley (whom you may wish to Google, as a very interesting character), has long since left us, but his work still remains, a reminder to us all of the early days, and the long lasting effect The Beatles and their music has had.

Scan the code with your smart-phone camera or QR Reader app to view the map, directions and more information.

4 Rodney Street
aka Brian Epstein's Birthplace
Liverpool L1 2TZ

It was at a private nursing home at this address that Queenie and Harry Epstein introduced their son, Brian Samuel, to the world, on 19th September 1934.

He was their first of two sons. His brother, Clive would follow 22 months later.

What a tragedy that such a brilliant young man only lived for 32 years.

It was a joyous moment for the parents, and Brian was born on Yom Kippur, (the Jewish Day of Atonement), a memorable day in their calendar.

The nursing home was considered the top of its class in Liverpool, in fact, the equivalent of the esteemed Harley Street in London.

Scan this code with your smart-phone camera or QR Reader app to view the map, directions and more information.

---

9 Madryn Street

aka Ringo's Birthplace

The Dingle, Liverpool   L8 3TT**PLEASE DO NOT DISTURB THE LOCAL RESIDENTS**

Madryn Street was Richard Starkey's first home. He was born here on July 7th, 1940 and lived here until he was 6. The family then moved a mere 2 blocks away to 10 Admiral Grove, close to the pub, The Empress, This pub, which adjoins the 2 streets, was featured on Ringo's album cover - *Sentimental Journey.* Over the years, the district has become run down and dilapidated, but still, Beatles fans like to visit the area, just for old time's sake, take pictures of the street sign and reminisce about what his early childhood might have been like for the future Sir Richard Starkey. The house has undergone many changes over the years, and is now just a memory.

The area was known as *The Welsh Streets,* because of their naming for Welsh towns, and at that time, consisted of about 450 Victorian houses.

Although the house is boarded up, the fans continue to write on the door and walls. The City Council decided against making it into a location of note, despite many protests from the locals.

Fab Four Taxi Tours shows photos of tourists, cameras in hand, who still want to visit the site, despite its dilapidated condition. How about you? Their phone number is +44 151-601-2111. Tell them Angie McCartney sent you. They took good care of us when we were in Liverpool for the launch of my first book, My Long and Winding Road.

The Madryn Street sign has had to be replaced many times, and currently its display, is a black back board covered in graffiti. A sad reflection of the times.

But you might still want to put it on your bucket list.

Scan this code with your smart-phone camera or QR Reader app to view the map, directions and more information.

Beatles Street Signs

Kensington, Liverpool 6, UK

PLEASE DO NOT DISTURB THE OCCUPANTS

In November 1981, The New York Times published an article saying that The Liverpool City Council had finally agreed to name streets after each of the Beatles. They are located in the Kensington District of Liverpool between Molyneux Rd, Coleridge Street, Kensington and Farnworth Streets, just east of Phythian Park, and are a nice tribute to the local lads.

They are just ordinary houses, with no particular claim to fame, other than their street names.

So as not to show favouritism, I list them alphabetically in order of surname:

George Harrison Close
Liverpool L6 9HY

John Lennon Drive
Liverpool L9 1HT

Paul McCartney Way
Liverpool L6 9HY

Ringo Starr Drive
Liverpool L6 9HY

Scan this code with your smart-phone camera or QR Reader app to view the map, directions and more information.

The Beatles Statue
Pier Head, Liverpool L3 1BY

An iconic statue of the Fab Four, in their hometown. The Beatles Statue arrived on Liverpool's Waterfront in December 2015. Donated by the famous Cavern Club, the placement of the statue coincides with the 50-year anniversary of the band's last gig played in Liverpool, at the Liverpool Empire Theatre. It was created by sculptor Andy Edwards.

Paul McCartney has a camera, maybe in a nod to his relationship with Linda Eastman.

John Lennon holds two acorns in his hand. In June of 1968, Yoko Ono and John Lennon planted two acorns in the garden of Coventry Cathedral, England. The seeds, they said, represented their wish for world peace. After marrying in 1969, the couple sent a pair of acorns to leaders across the world asking that the "living sculptures" be planted as a symbol of world peace.

Ringo Starr has the number '8' printed on the sole of his boot. The '8' references L8, his childhood Postcode in Liverpool.

George Harrison has Sanskrit writing on the belt of his coat. Let ME know if you find out what it says!

Scan the code with your smart-phone camera or QR Reader app to view the map, directions and more information.

Blackler's Store

53 Great Charlotte Street Liverpool L1, UK

Original Tel: "Royal" (709) 6260 - yes, they had words for telephone exchanges in those days!!!

Blackler's Store was one of Liverpool's finest, a multi story emporium, based on The Lafayette in Paris and I have very happy memories of sitting on Santa's lap (and remembering him smelling of beer), when I was but a little tot. Mum used to take me there every year, (except in 1941 when it was bombed), and in fact, I carried on the tradition when Ruth was a young 'un. I have a delightful photograph of she and her Cousin Geraldine on one of these memorable occasions.

It had a huge glass dome at the top and a permanent blow up Santa. If you scan the code on the next page, will find a 1968/69 Christmas Grotto documentary on Youtube.com – Blackler's Department Store, narrated by Ken Dodd, Liverpool's much beloved comedian.

But its real claim to fame is that George Harrison once worked there. After he failed to make the grade with his exams at The Liverpool Institute, in an effort to get some kind of job without any qualifications, the job centre sent him to Blackler's, where they needed a window dresser.

Unfortunately, by the time he got his interview, that post had been filled, and they offered him a job as an apprentice electrician, so he took it.

George is quoted as saying "So I got a job cleaning all the lights with a paint brush, all those tubes to keep clean, and at Christmas, I kept the Grotto clean." Little did he imagine what the future held for him. But by the age of 17, he was able to tell his boss he would be leaving to go on tour to Scotland, backing Johnny Gentle. The shop has since been changed into a slew of smaller and varied retail premises.

Scan this code with your smart-phone camera or QR Reader app to view the map, video, directions and more information.

The Brian Epstein Statue
Whitechapel, Liverpool

This (IMHO) long-overdue statue co-sculpted by designers Andy Edwards and my great-niece, talented artist Jane Robbins (whose parents Bette and Mike introduced me to to Jim McCartney in August 1964), have created a wonderful homage to the "power behind the throne" as some, including my step-son Sir Paul have also called him "The 5th Beatle."

At the time of writing, the destination is still being planned by the Town Hall and City elders, it is going to be placed adjacent to the Epstein family business NEMS, with Brian pointing towards Mathew Street and The Cavern. It's sure to become one of Liverpool's most "Instagrammable" spots. Scan the code to learn more.

The Liverpool College of Art
68 Hope St, Liverpool L1 7AY
Tel: 44 151-330-3000

In early 2012, the College was purchased by LIPA (The Liverpool Institute for Performing Arts) for GBP 3.7 million as they wished to expand their range of services offered to include dance tuition, and a studio theatre.

Mark Featherstone-Witty, LIPA CEO and co-founding Principal (along with Paul McCartney), is quoted as saying at the time that "There are sound business reasons why we are buying the College of Art, but there's no denying the romance of bringing together two buildings where three Beatles once did their learning.

The notables he was referring to are Art School students John Lennon and Stuart Sutcliffe, and of course Paul himself at "The Inny."

In addition, Cynthia Powell (the future Mrs. John Lennon) studied at the College, along with famed Liverpool writer Bill Harry, and Derek Taylor, one time Beatles Publicist and Head of Warner Brothers, UK.

Scan this code with your smart-phone camera or QR Reader app to view the map, video, directions and more information.

Dovedale Primary School

Herondale Rd, Liverpool L18 1JX,

Tel: +44 151 733 4232

This school lays claim to fame of several people who went on to be stars in the entertainment world. It was established in 1908.

John Lennon attended from 1945 to 1951, George Harrison between 1948 and 1950, and Jimmy Tarbuck, the famous Liverpool comedian also attended Dovedale.

George was three years younger than John, so they were not there at the same time, Now, wouldn't that have started something? There is nothing on record that tells if they ever knew one another at that stage of their lives.

Pete Sissons was another scholar, and he turned out to be one of John's few life long friends who went on to be a bigwig at the BBC in London.

The School has undergone some financial difficulties over the years, and in 2001, Yoko donated $250,000 to help with repairs of the ageing property.

Scan the code on the next page with your smart-phone camera or QR Reader app to view the map, video, directions and more info.

Eleanor Rigby's Grave
St Peter's Churchyard, Woolton, Liverpool
Tel: +44 151 428 6810

The gravestone of one Eleanor Rigby who died on October 10th 1939, aged 44, can be found in the churchyard of St. Peter's in Woolton, the very place where John and Paul first met in July of 1957.

In August 1966, The Beatles released the single Eleanor Rigby the B-side of Yellow Submarine, it was also included on the Album Revolver. The song was composed by Paul McCartney and since the release the question has always been asked of Paul, "Who is Eleanor Rigby?" Paul later recalled that he must have seen the name subliminally when they would go across from the church hall to the graveyard to smoke ciggies and hang out. He was not consciously aware of such a person.

Also interred in this cemetery are the remains of Julia Lennon, John's biological mother, and Stuart Sutcliffe, the early Beatle who died in Germany but who was brought back to Liverpool for final interment at the wishes of his family.

Scan the code on the next page with your smart-phone camera or QR Reader app to view the map, video, directions and more info.

Eleanor Rigby Statue
34 Stanley Street, Liverpool L1 6AL

When Tommy Steele, the popular London performer, was appearing at the Liverpool Empire in 1981, he decided he would like to make a sculpture as a tribute to The Beatles, and hit on the idea of a piece about Eleanor Rigby, to commemorate their song of the same name.

He approached the City Council, who were delighted to accept his offer, and he said his fee would be three-pence. This was because he had originally achieved success in the West End stage show *"Half a Sixpence"*.

The council decided to make a donation of 4,000 GBP towards the cost of the endeavour.

It took him nine months to build it, and he eventually unveiled it in Liverpool on 3rd December 1982.

It is a charming piece, depicting a lady sitting on a bench, purse on her lap, and a shopping bag beside her on the bench, and sticking out slightly is a bottle of milk.

Beside her is a copy of The Liverpool Echo, and perched on the newspaper is a little bird with a piece of bread.

A plaque next to the monument dedicates it 'To All The Lonely People' Of course, Eleanor Rigby is a fictional character, although a grave was found near St Peter's Church in Woolton (where Paul met John) with the name Eleanor Rigby on it.

It is a very popular piece of the Liverpool scene and was, as they suspected, a terrific boost to Liverpool Tourism, which at that time was nothing like as huge as it is now.

Scan this code with your smart-phone camera or QR Reader app to view the map, video, directions and more information.

Ferry 'Cross The Mersey
Liverpool Pier Head

The Mersey Ferry is a ferry service operating on the River Mersey in north west England, between Liverpool to the east and Birkenhead and Wallasey on the Wirral Peninsula to the west.

Ferries have been used on this route since at least the 12th century, and continue to be popular for both locals and visitors.

It became known worldwide when Gerry Marsden recorded his song: "Ferry 'Cross The Mersey."

I used to ride The Royal Iris in my young days, between the Pier Head and Wallasey Ferry, where I would visit relatives. I had a posh Aunty in Wallasey. Aunty Dolly. The kind of person who had grapes on the sideboard when nobody was sick. And lace curtains.

One particular Ferry Boat (known as The Dazzle), whose real name is SNOWDROP, was refurbished and glorified by the great artist Sir Peter Blake, designer of the Sgt Pepper cover.

You can find current information in that great publication: The Guide, Liverpool. It will keep you up-to-date with availability of visits to this and many other attractions on both sides of the River Mersey.

You can even have a nice cuppa tea at The Fab 4 Cafe in the terminus while you wait for the next Ferry.

Scan this code with your smart-phone camera or QR Reader app to view the map, directions and more information.

Hessy's Music Centre

62 Stanley Street, Liverpool, United Kingdom

Frank Hessy and his business partner Jim Gretty ran an instrument shop in the City Centre, where most of the local musicians bought their gear.

There were other, bigger stores, Like Rushworth's and Crane's, but little old Hessy's remained the local favourite. Also, Hessy's extended The Beatles credit, and this is where, in 1957 John Lennon bought his first guitar for £17. It was also partly because Frank made them so welcome, let them noodle around on his stock items, and they were like one big happy family.

Frank founded a little magazine called "Frank Comments," and all of the young up-and-coming struggling artists would avidly pounce on every issue, to see if they got a mention. This publication was written by the local music aficionado Bill Harry, a student at Liverpool Art College, who of course, went on to found the famous *Mersey Beat Magazine*.

Bill also authored a magnificent book called *The Ultimate Beatles Encyclopedia*, which, to this day, remains, along with the amazing publications of Mark Lewisohn, a reliable source of reference on what was happening in Liverpool's music scene at that time.

It was published in 1992, and many dog-eared copies of it are still on the bookshelves of music lovers and students everywhere.

Myself included.

Scan this code with your smart-phone camera or QR Reader app to view the map, video, directions and more information.

John Lennon Airport
Speke Hall Ave, Speke, Liverpool L24 1YD
Tel: +44 871 521 8484

Originally known as Speke Airport, it was re-dedicated to the memory of John Lennon in 2001. It was the first British Airport to be named after an individual.

It has grown into a popular International Terminal, with many attractions for the Beatles' fans, including artwork, shopping destinations, and a prominent sculpture at the entrance. Many people go there just to buy souvenirs, and for the photo op. Even if they are not travelling.

On the roof is painted the airport's motto, a line from Lennon's song "*Imagine*": "Above us, only sky." In 2005 the *Yellow Submarine*, a large-scale work of art, was installed on a traffic island at the entrance to the airport. A permanent exhibition of The Beatles in India's photographs made in 1968 at the Ashram of Maharishi Mahesh Yogi, (founder of the Transcendental Meditation technique), by Paul Saltzman, can be seen above the retail units in the departure lounge.

They also run charter flights to several remote destinations, so if you are feeling adventurous, or maybe have won the lottery, give them a call and see what they have to offer.

Scan this code with your smart-phone camera or QR Reader app to view the map, directions and more information.

Joseph Williams Primary School
Sunnyfield Rd, Netherley, Liverpool L25 2NB
NOW CLOSED

When The Stockton Wood School became overcrowded, young brothers Paul and Michael McCartney were moved to Joseph Williams Primary School in Netherley.

This meant a half hour bus ride from where they were living in Speke, but the lads seemed to enjoy their travel time. It was a newly built school in a preservation area, so it was a nice change for them.

The boys had a great relationship with their headmaster, whom they called "Pop." At this stage in his life, Paul had put on weight, and was unhappy as the kids started calling him "fatty."

However, he was a good student and didn't have any problems passing his exams, qualifying him to become a pupil at The Liverpool Institute. He was a pupil at Joseph Williams from 1949 to 1953.

Scan this code with your smart-phone camera or QR Reader app to view the map, directions and more information.

Lewis's Store

Liverpool L2 2LZ, Liverpool

NOW AN APARTMENT BUILDING

Like Blackler's Stores, Lewis's was another of the great iconic department stores that epitomises the spirit, humour and unity of a City like Liverpool.

It was originated in 1856 by David Lewis, mainly dealing in men's and boys' clothing. Then in time, it branched out into women's clothing later adding various other departments, including shoes in 1874, then tobacco in 1879, thought at the time to be very risqué.

Just across the street from the famed Adelphi Hotel, it stood out as a beacon of the pride of the City, and despite being bombed almost to extinction during world War II, it rose again from the ashes, and after many years of reconstruction, almost returned to its former glory.

When it reopened, the public was shocked, outraged, delighted, and amused by the statue that adorned it's facade. Fondly known as "Dicky Lewis" it was a nude man, proudly displaying all of his attributes. And over the years, it became famous as a meeting place, when people would say, "I'll meet you under Dicky Lewis."

It was a favourite meeting place of John and Cynthia, and she would be embarrassed, standing under this statue, usually in the sexy attire that John demanded, fishnet tights, short skirts and high-heeled shoes.

That was not the real Cynthia, but how John wanted her to be. And she loved him so much that in those early days, she never dared refuse him.

The Beatles performed at a special event on the top floor of the store on 28th November 1962. This was a private event for a staff event for The 527 Club, billed as "The Young Idea Dance."

Peter Brown, later to be Brian Epstein's Personal Assistant, was Manager of their record Department.

It finally closed its doors in early 2010. Many a Scouser bade Dicky a fond farewell. Scan this code with your smart-phone camera or QR Reader app to view the map, directions and more information.

Linda McCartney Centre

Royal Liverpool & Broadgreen University Hospital, Prescot St, Liverpool L7 8XP, UK
Tel: +44 151 706 2000

The Linda McCartney Centre, a part of the Royal Liverpool Hospitals system, is a treatment centre dedicated to Paul's late wife, the mother of Heather, Mary, Stella and James.

A retrospective of Linda's work had been planned from August 8th to November 1st 2020 at The Walker Art Gallery in Liverpool's City Centre. Curated by Paul, Mary and Stella, consisting of over 200 photographs, including a selection of images of Liverpool itself.

It is regretted that, due to the outbreak of the Pandemic, this event had to be postponed, and it is hoped to reschedule it at a later date.

This information will be publicized as soon as it becomes available.

Linda is memorialized, and leaves behind a body of work to draw attention to the cause, and hopefully help to find a cure and give hope to the many people who use the facilities of this magnificent centre.

I had the personal pleasure of visiting the centre during my time in Liverpool in 2013, and actually meeting patients undergoing chemotherapy, who were very vocal in their praise of the treatment they were receiving, and I personally have three friends who have been cured of cancer due to early detection and excellent attention here.

Donations are always welcome, no matter how small, and you can be sure that when they find a cure, they will share it with the world.

Mendips
251 Menlove Avenue, Woolton, Liverpool UK

This is the childhood home of John Lennon. Located in the Woolton suburb of Liverpool, it is nicknamed Mendips after the Mendip Hills. The Grade II listed building is preserved by the National Trust.

The 1933-built home belonged to John Lennon's Aunt Mimi and her husband George Smith. It is in Woolton, South Liverpool. Lennon moved there in July 1946 at the age of 5 from 9 Newcastle Road in the nearby suburb of Wavertree.

He lived at Mendips after his mother, who was living with her boyfriend, was persuaded that it would be better for his Aunt Mimi and George to take care of him.

The house is very closely situated to the original Strawberry Field where he and a childhood friend, Pete Shotton, used to climb over the wall after Salvation Army events and collect beer bottles to return them for the penny deposit.

He remained at Mendips until mid-1963, when he was 22 years old.

It was approximately 30 metres north west of this house that Lennon's Mother Julia was hit by a car and killed on the evening of 15 July, 1958.

In 1965, Mimi sold the property, taking away some of the furnishings and giving away others.

Yoko eventually purchased the house and donated it to the National Trust to preserve its legacy from an historical point of view.

Scan the code with your smart-phone camera or QR Reader app to view the map, directions and more information.

Mersey Beat Magazine
NOW CLOSED
81a Renshaw St, Liverpool L1 2SJ, United Kingdom
Tel: +44 151 707 1805

I know this is a publication, rather than a location, but it has played such an integral part of the Mersey scene throughout its emergence, that I thought you would at least like to know more about it. Today there's a cozy little Cafe called 81 Records which holds up the tradition as a coffee bar and record shop with open mics and live music.

It was the brainchild of Bill Harry, who was there right from the beginning. He worked in the midst of it all, writing reviews and generally supporting the Liverpool scene.

Bill Harry was a student at The Liverpool College of Art, and began by writing for Frank Hessy's music column, and progressed to starting his own publication, with the help of a 50 quid funding from Dick Mathews, whom he met at The Jacaranda Coffee Club.

Bill Harry

They rented a little office above a Wine Merchant's shop (now 81 Records) at 81 Renshaw Street. Bill's Assistant was his girlfriend Virginia (now his wife of many years), presumably unpaid! Doing it for love instead of money.

They distributed 5,000 copies of their first edition in July 1961, and distributed it via various music stores and book shops. Brian Epstein evidently ordered 12 copies of the first edition, and it sold out in no time, So by edition 2, he needed 12 dozen copies, and they knew they were on their way.

Poor Virginia was swamped, and evidently, the Beatles themselves would drop by the office from time to time to help her out, answering phones etc.

The Beatles were strongly featured in every issue, with photographs supplied by Paul's brother Mike McCartney.

As time went on, various business troubles muddied the waters, and it eventually merged with another London entity, and finally disappeared. But Scousers, and music lovers everywhere will always regard it as a very important part of the early history of the Mersey scene.

Scan this code with your smart-phone camera or QR Reader app to view the map, directions and more information.

Mount Pleasant Registry Office
NOW CLOSED
64 Mount Pleasant, Liverpool L3 5RY, UK

This Grade II listed Georgian property, 62 Mount Pleasant, was originally built for merchant William Rice in 1767. Mount Pleasant is one of the oldest properties in Liverpool, and one of the oldest buildings in the street. Next door, at N°64 was formally the registry office where John Lennon married first wife Cynthia on August 23rd, 1962.

Brian Epstein was their best man. Paul McCartney and George Harrison also attended. John's Aunt Mimi did not, as she was not in favour of the marriage. After the ceremony, the party ran down the hill, in the rain, for a wedding breakfast at Reece's Cafe, hosted by Brian. *(See separate chapter for more about this feast).*

Earlier, on April 17th 1954, Ringo's Mum married Harry Graves there. A second marriage for both. He legally adopted Ritchie (Ringo), and they became one really happy family.

Scan this code with your smart-phone camera or QR Reader app to view the map, directions and more information.

NEMS (aka North End Music Stores)
Epstein & Sons, Walton Road, Liverpool
NEMS), Charlotte Street, Liverpool
NEMS, Whitechapel, Liverpool
NEMS, 24 Moorfield, Liverpool
and finally,

NEMS Argyle Street, London

Brian's parents, Harry and Queenie Epstein originally owned the family business. (Queenie was Harry's pet name for his wife, whose name was Malka, which means "Queen").

It originally began as a furniture store on Walton Road, (in the North End of Liverpool), when it was called Epstein & Sons. and later progressed to selling pianos and sheet music.

In fact, my late husband, Jim McCartney (Paul and Michael's Dad) bought an upright piano from them.

That must have been a huge decision for him in those early days of financial hardship, but his great love of music overcame his fiscal awareness, so anxious was he that his two sons should always be surrounded by music. How right he turned out to be, with both of the boys being so incredibly talented.

When Harry and Queenie decided to expand further, they opened another branch, known as NEMS, (North End Music Stores) in Charlotte Street, closer to the City Centre.

Brian and his brother Clive were appointed to run this shop, which was doing well, encouraging them to open yet another branch, this time mainly a record shop in Whitechapel, again in the City Centre. Brian and Clive were really keen to become established in that particular branch.

It had listening booths where potential clients could listen to their favourite records through headphones. These booths resembled little telephone booths, but without doors. They became very popular with the youngsters, who would crowd in during their lunch hours and after work until closing time.

Brian's entrepreneurial streak led him to register many more companies in the NEMS Empire, including a theatrical booking agency, and once more, the company eventually opened new offices at 24 Moorfield in August of 1963. This is where ultimately, The Beatles, Gerry and The Pacemakers, Cilla Black and artists such as Billy J. Kramer were signed up, and their careers began to move forward.

They then began a Concert Promotion arm, and moved to Sutherland House, Argyle Street, London. Brian wanted fan club secretary and Girl Friday Freda Kelly to move with them, but her Father was against the idea, as she was so young.

Instead, he moved her from being his personal Secretary to being The Beatles Fan Club Secretary, a story which is aptly documented in the award winning DVD called "Good Ol' Freda."

I am very proud to say that Freda invited me to take part in this piece of history. I was "ready for my close up" for sure!

There was some discussion at one time that The Beatles should buy NEMS, but it seems that Linda's father, lawyer Lee Eastman had some reservations about that, and the arrangement never came to fruition.

This was around the time that Alan Klein came on the scene, and as every Beatles aficionado knows, things were just never the same after that.

Scan the code on the next page with your smart-phone camera or QR Reader app to view the map, directions and more information.

Penny Lane
Penny Lane Development Trust
70 Penny Lane, Liverpool L18 1BW
Development Trust
Tel: +44 151 733 7245

Most tourist help and information can be obtained from The Penny Lane Development Trust, which lovingly curates memorabilia and artifacts relating to The Beatles, in particular, paying homage to their recording of Penny Lane - originally a bus depot.

There you can see photographs of the barber (who shaved another customer), to the pretty nurse who sold poppies from a tray. It is run by a lovely lady, Julie Gornell, who makes everyone welcome and is always happy to answer your questions.

It's a busy thoroughfare, with not 1, but 2 street signs, which have survived much graffiti over the years and are probably amongst the most photographed signs in the world. Please don't steal them!

Scan this code with your smart-phone camera or QR Reader app to view the map, directions and more information.

Quarry Bank School

24 Harthill Road, Calderstones, Liverpool L18 3HS

Tel: +44 151-724-2087

This is the school John Lennon attended. It is now called The Calderstones School, a co-educational comprehensive school, in the Liverpool suburb of Allerton.

It began life as Quarry Bank High School for boys in 1922. When John was a pupil there from 1952, he got together with a few friends and formed his first band, The Quarrymen.

The school song was *The Song of the Quarry*, which prompted him to give the band their name.

They would sing it every morning, and the first few lines were:

> *Quarry men old before our birth*
> *Straining each muscle and sinew*
> *Toiling together Mother earth*
> *Conquered the rock that was in you.*

The other members of The Quarrymen were: Pete Shotton, Ron Davis, Len Garry, Colin Hanton and Eric Griffiths. It's generally considered that John Lennon was the only one who took it seriously. The others were in it just for fun.

In July 1957, along came Paul McCartney, and a bit later, George Harrison, and then Stuart Sutcliffe. But by the time Stuart joined them, the band had changed their lineup. And by this time, John had moved on to Art College and lost touch with most of his earlier school friends.

Then when Ivan Vaughan introduced his friend, Paul McCartney, John is quoted as having said: "That was the day. The day that I met Paul, that it started moving."

It sure did.

Scan the code on the next page with your smart-phone camera or QR Reader app to view the map, directions and more information.

Reece's Café and Ballroom
John & Cynthia's Wedding Reception Location
Corner of Parker Street and Leigh Street, Liverpool L1

My recollections of Reece's Café was that it was rather upscale, with a grocery store on the ground floor, a Café upstairs, and a Ballroom on the top floor, where they would hold Wednesday and Saturday afternoon Tea Dances, to which I was very partial in my younger days. It was a great place to meet boys who actually wore collars and ties.

We were very proper in those days, many ladies wearing hats, gloves, and twirly skirts. We were accompanied by a live band. I think the price of admission was about a shilling.

When John Lennon married Cynthia Powell in a secret ceremony on August 23rd 1962, Brian Epstein (the Best Man for the occasion) said he would *"take care of everything"*. Paul and George also attended. In fact, when the officiant asked for the groom to step forward, George, to break the ice, did so causing giggles all round.

And so it was, off to Reece's...Brian had forgotten to book a table, so they were kept waiting in the lobby for about twenty minutes before being seated. It was busy with lunchtime local office workers.

Incidentally, Reece's was where John's parents Alf and Julia had also celebrated their own wedding in 1938.

The guests in 1963 included Paul and George, and they all sat down and tucked in to a hearty meal. Menu:

      Soup
      Chicken
      Trifle

A repast fit for a king!

The restaurant didn't have an alcohol license at the time, so Brian toasted the Bride and Groom in water. And when Brian paid the bill, it totalled fifteen shillings, i.e. 75 pence per head. Ahhh … the good old days.

Scan this code with your smart-phone camera or QR Reader app to view the map, directions and more information.

Rushworth & Dreaper's Music Store
NOW CLOSED

72 St Anne Street, Liverpool, L3 3DY UK

Rushworth and Dreaper's store was originally primarily an organ building company which began creating organs for International places of worship, from little Parish Churches to Cathedrals in the 1800's, In later years, they progressed to being a general supplier of musical instruments. Today it is the home of Henry Willis & Sons, still an instrument manufacturer.

In fact, I once attended a course in Jazz Piano Music there at The Billy Mayerl School of Music in my teens. It was a very old fashioned place, almost like a church in those days, with a very prim receptionist inside the front door, who would direct you to the department of your choice. She always spoke in hushed tones, and made you feel as though you should genuflect before speaking to her. Or at least look around for a holy water font. She must have been shocked when someone, seeking the piano department, asked her:

"Where do I go to get felt?"

Jim McCartney bought a trumpet from Rushworth's, then Europe's largest music house, and also somewhere that would allow him to exchange the instrument for a £25 German guitar.

"The story goes that Paul couldn't play it because he was left handed so he had to turn the strings round the other way", Jonathan Rushworth, great-great grandson of Rushworth's founder recalls.

The Beatles' connection with the store continued when, in September 1962, having just secured their first recording contract, John Lennon and George Harrison bought 2 Gibson guitars, imported from Chicago. Never a man to miss an opportunity, Jonathan's father, James Rushworth ensured a camera was on hand to capture the presentation. The photograph, in which Harrison sports the remnants of a black eye sustained in a Pete Best-related Cavern scuffle, hung on the shop wall for decades.

Scan this code with your smart-phone camera or QR Reader app to view the map, directions and more information.

Sefton General Hospital
NOW CLOSED
Smithdown Road, Liverpool L15

Sefton General Hospital was originally part of Toxteth Park Workhouse, which was part of the West Derby Union. In 1930 the Union was disbanded due to the abolition of the poor law, and the hospital, which was now administered by Liverpool Corporation, changed its name to Smithdown Road Infirmary.

Sefton General was an NHS (public) hospital where John's Mother Julia Lennon was taken after being a victim in a road accident and was pronounced DOA on July 15th, 1958.

John was 17 years old at the time, and he was at Julia's house at 17 Bloomfield Road when a policeman came to tell him and John Dykins, (Julia's boyfriend) that she had been involved in an accident but did not tell them of the outcome.

The two immediately rushed there in a taxi, to learn the distressing news. This was the hospital where Julia's two daughters by Dykins had also been born, Julia and Jacqueline. Dykins himself died there in 1969, another victim of a road accident.

Then on 8th April 1963, Cynthia Lennon gave birth to son Julian in that same hospital. John was on tour at the time, but it was a very difficult birth, with the umbilical cord being wrapped around Julian's neck.

It is said that, when John finally visited his wife and son, he held him in his arms and said: "*Who's going to be a famous little rocker like his Dad then?*" How right he was. Julian is an incredibly talented, philanthropic, loving and all round wonderful guy, whom I am proud to call my friend.

St. Barnabas Church

Smithdown Place, Near Penny Lane, Liverpool L18 6JJ

St Barnabas church is located across from the famous Penny Lane roundabout made famous by John Lennon and McCartney. Paul McCartney attended and was in the choir at this church made famous by the Beatles. Paul pointed it out on a drive by with US talk show host James Corden in his Carpool Karaoke segment on Liverpool. If you scan the code with this entry, you can watch the video.

Paul made another appearance in more recent times, when he was best man at the wedding of his brother Michael, to Rowena Horne in 1982. This Church is beautiful and has a calming effect on one when you enter. And it is doubly interesting, of course, because of its Beatles connections.

They periodically open up the bell tower, when you can go to the top and have an amazing view of the entire City.

A truly worthwhile photo op for the Day Tripper. And so close to visit while you are at Penny Lane.

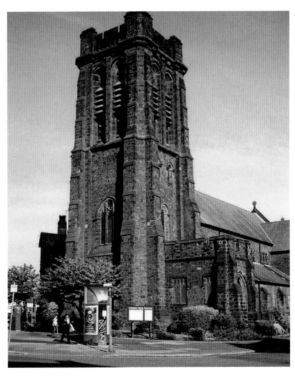

Scan the code on the next page with your smart-phone camera or QR Reader app to view the map, directions and more information.

St. Peter's Church

Church Road, Woolton Village, Liverpool

Email: parishadmin@stpeters-woolton.org.uk

St. Peter's is an Anglican Parish Church, listed in the National Heritage List of England as a Grade II listed building. It is one of the biggest Parish Churches in Liverpool. It's bell tower stands at the highest point in the City.

It is also famed for its Beatles connections, as it was there, at a Church Fete, that the historic first meeting of John Lennon and Paul McCartney took place on 6th July 1957 when The Quarrymen, (the forerunner of The Beatles) performed. It is where the gravestone of Eleanor Rigby rests, she who was immortalised in song in the famous composition written and performed by Paul McCartney.

The 2020 Pandemic saw them convert to virtual services, remaining a lively and active Parish, all ages welcome, and lots of social activities in addition to regular services.

Scan this code with your smart-phone camera or QR Reader app to view the map, directions and more information.

Strawberry Field

Beaconsfield Road, Liverpool L25 6EJ

Tel: +44 151 252 6130

It was originally a Salvation Army property and visitor attraction in the Liverpool suburb of Woolton. It operated as a children's home between 1936 and 2005. The house and grounds had originally been built as a private residence in the Victorian era, before being acquired by the Salvation Army in the 1930s. The house was demolished in 1973 due to structural problems and replaced with purpose-built units. After being closed as a children's home, it continued to be used by the Salvation Army for fundraising and social purposes.

John Lennon lived nearby on Menlove Avenue with his Aunty Mimi, and used to climb over the wall after various celebrations and 'nick' empty lemonade and beer bottles and take them to the local sweet shop to retrieve the one penny deposit per bottle, and use it to buy ciggies. You could buy them one at a time in those days, they were known as a "loosie." I remember that as a little kid, my brother Bob used to send me to our local shop to buy him a "loosie." Age was not a condition of a sale in those days. I was probably about 6 or 7 years old.

In more recent times, it became the theme for John's popular song, *Strawberry Fields Forever.* Its gates have been subjected to so much graffiti that during the recent refurbishment of the property, the new gates were treated with an anti-graffiti substance which it is hoped will make them retain their pristine condition.

Scheduled to re-open to the public as a tourist attraction in late 2020, when my step-son Mike McGear McCartney has announced plans to celebrate the occasion with the release of a new book of photography.

Scan this code with your smart-phone camera or QR Reader app to view the map, directions and more information.

The Adelphi Hotel
Ranelagh St, Liverpool L3 5UL
Tel: +44 151-709-7200

The Adelphi is Liverpool's most famous hotel. It had its heyday when the luxury liners would sail into the Port with their rich passengers, and the hotel's accommodations and the meals were luxurious and very expensive. It later served as the hub for International Beatle Week every August.

It originally opened in 1826. The present hotel is the third one on this site. It's a seven-storey building and has welcomed as its guests over the years many celebrities, including Sir Winston Churchill, Franklin D. Roosevelt, Judy Garland, Bob Dylan, Frank Sinatra, and Roy Rogers, who once rode his horse "Trigger" into the Lobby. And of course, The Beatles.

My Uncle, Willy Conlon, who had two Opticians businesses in Liverpool, Conlon and Sons, and lived "over the water" in Heswall, rented a permanent suite there, to stay overnight when he was kept late at the office, and was treated royally as a semi-resident. I can remember visiting him there, and being astonished at the luxury, the service, the towels, oh, the towels, they seemed a mile thick to me.

Scan this code with your smart-phone camera or QR Reader app to view the map, directions and more information.

The Beatles Story Museum
Royal Quay, Liverpool, England L3 4AD
Tel: +44 151 709 1963

The Beatles Story Museum, owned and operated by Mersey Travel, is located on the historical Royal Albert Dock, and was opened on 1st May 1990.

The Beatles Story contains re-creations of Mona Best's Casbah Coffee Club, The Cavern Club, located just a few blocks away on Mathew Street, John & Yoko's music room, and Abbey Road Studios, among other historical Beatles items, such as John Lennon's glasses, George Harrison's first guitar, one of Ringo's rare Ludwig Drum Kits, toys, memorabilia, collectibles and a detailed history about the solo careers of each of the Fab Four. The museum was recognised as one of the best tourist attractions of the United Kingdom in 2015.

This space contains some amazing examples of the history of The Beatles. You can also grab a bite at their Fab4 Cafe. This is on the "must do" list for any Liverpool visit.

Scan this code with your smart-phone camera or QR Reader app to view the map, directions and more information.

The Blue Angel Nightclub
106-108 Seel Street, Liverpool L1 4BL, United Kingdom
Tel: +44 151 709 1535

The Blue Angel was a popular coffee bar, owned by Allan Williams, The Beatles' first manager, and it's where the boys would hang out and fantasize about their musical aspirations and dreams.

It became a popular "hang" as the boys gathered fans, and they would pitch in and help Allan get the place ship shape for their nighttime customers.

Pete Best's audition to join the Beatles took place in the Blue Angel on 12th August 1960. It was also where the Beatles, in 1960, auditioned for impresario Larry Parnes landing them their first tour outside Liverpool, supporting singer Johnny Gentle on a tour of Scotland.

After hearing Cilla Black perform "Bye Bye Blackbird" at the Blue Angel, her eventual manager Brian Epstein contracted Black as his only female client on 6th September 1963.

Its nickname was "The Raz" and in the early 60's, lots of up-and-coming muzos played there, including Bob Dylan, The Rolling Stones and The Beatles. It was a happy, if scruffy sort of place. Cheap drinks, loud music, and happy people. And lots of ciggies. But no drugs in those early days.

Scan this code with your smart-phone camera or QR Reader app to view the map, directions and more information.

The Casbah Coffee Club

8 Hayman's Green Liverpool L12 7JG United Kingdom
Tel: +44 151-280-3519

The Casbah was started by the Beatles' first Drummer, Pete Best's Mother, Mona Best, in the cellar of her 15 bedroom family home. Mona was born in India, as was Pete, and the story goes that she won some money on a horse race and invested in the house. Once Mona returned to Liverpool, it all changed.

After seeing a TV show about the 2i's Coffee Bar in London, she came up with the idea of making her basement into a place where Pete and his friends could get together and play music. In the early days, The Quarrymen, (John Lennon, Paul McCartney, George Harrison and Ken Brown) had their first booking there. Mona said that they must first help her paint the cellar, and they painted spiders, dragons, rainbows and stars.

Art student Cynthia Powell, (not yet married to John Lennon) painted a silhouette of John on the wall which still can be seen today. It was a members only club, making it a tad exclusive.

In 2006, Culture Minister David Lammy pronounced it a Grade II building, listed by the British Heritage Society. The Casbah celebrated its 60th Anniversary in August 2019, and in 2020, announced plans to become a bed and breakfast, which opened in late 2021.

Roag Best (Pete's younger brother) and his team have put their hearts and souls into the renovation project, and you can follow them on Facebook @ casbahcoffeclub.

"The Casbah was the place where all that started. We looked upon it as our personal club." Sir Paul McCartney.

The Casbah Coffee Club is the only original Beatles venue to remain unchanged.

The Casbah's many original features include,
Aztec Room - Aztec motif ceiling painted by John Lennon.
Rainbow Room - Original stage area used by The Quarrymen with rainbow ceiling painted by Sir Paul McCartney.
Spider Room - Original stage used by The Beatles & many other Mersey Beat stars.
Star Ceiling - painted by Pete, John, Paul, George & Stuart Sutcliffe.
Dragon, spider & spider web - painted by Pete & Mona Best.
Silhouette of John Lennon - painted by Cynthia Lennon.
Tours of The Casbah are available by pre-arranged bookings only.

Find out more, including a link to the GPS coordinates and background history by scanning this code with your phone or iPad camera:

The Cavern
10 Mathew St, Liverpool L2 6RE
Tel: +44 151 236 9091

The Cavern in Mathew Street Liverpool needs no introduction. Not since The Beatles began their career there. It has lived through many changes, including a change of address, but has become known worldwide as a mecca for tourists.

In the early 60's I used to sneak there in my lunch times to listen to the exciting music of the many Mersey bands, including The Beatles, never dreaming that I would become a part of their extended family when I married Jim McCartney, Paul's Dad, in November 1964.

When you visit, be sure to tell Jon Keats, Bill Heckle or Phil Winstanley that Angie McCartney sent you. As you'd expect, it is down a set of steps, leading to an authentic re-creation of the magical place where it all began.

Tourists tend to write their names on the walls, when they can find a space. It has an atmosphere that you cannot explain until you have visited.

In the early days, the kids would line up in Mathew Street, hoping to get in before they reached their maximum capacity. They'd move the rows of chairs to make room for them to dance, they called it The Cavern Stomp.

Group after group would take the tiny stage, belt out their music, many cover tunes, and then The Beatles began playing their own compositions, which was a brand new idea.

Then, once they had been on The Ed Sullivan Show in New York, their world, (and ours) changed. I urge you to feel the vibe of The Cavern. You'll never forget it.

Scan this code with your smart-phone camera or QR Reader app to view the map, directions and more information.

The Liverpool Empire Theatre
Lime St, Liverpool L1 1JE
Tel: +44 844-871-3017

The Liverpool Empire's history dates back to 1925, and has undergone many changes of ownership and style throughout the years.

Liverpool was delighted that The Beatles had performed there in their early days. I have a fond recollection of seeing Roy Rogers actually ride into the Lobby on Trigger, his trusty steed. I don't know if they had a stable for him (the horse) backstage, or who took care of him while his Master was on stage.

The Quarrymen first appeared there when they auditioned for the Carroll Levis Talent show: *Search for the Stars*. They didn't win on that occasion, but later re-entered the contest, calling themselves Johnny and The Moon Dogs. This time they got as far as the finals, which were held in Manchester.

The Beatles made their first appearance in October 1962 in a production co-produced by NEMS and Ray McFall of The Cavern. There were two shows that evening and The Beatles were the third act onstage.

In March 1963, they were back on the bill supporting Chris Montez and Tommy Roe, and on the afternoon of 7th December 1963 they filmed a special edition of *Juke Box Jury*, and later the same day, filmed another BBC show called *It's The Beatles*.

Their final show at The Liverpool Empire was on 5th December 1965, by which time they were famous, and there were over 10,000 ticket requests. That was the last time they played in Liverpool as The Beatles. Paul McCartney would return on May 18th 1973 with WINGS - you can see the set list by scanning the code below with your smart phone.

The Empress Pub

93 High Park Street, Liverpool L8 3UF

Tel: +44 151-726-0159

The Empress pub is located very close to where Ringo Starr lived as a child. In fact, he used it as the Album cover for his Sentimental Journey CD.

As it is to be expected, it proudly boasts pictures of the boy himself, along with his workmates, and has various other bits and bobs of memorabilia dotted around the place.

It is a favourite hangout of many locals, who always welcome tourists and are happy to tell them stories of "the old days."

Ringo's Mum, Elsie worked there at one time, in the days when it was essential for her to bring in some extra pennies to feed her growing boy. Little did she know then what the future was to hold.

Elsie once showed me a Post Office savings book where she would regularly deposit a few bob from the allowance her son had begun making her when The Beatles first started their rise to fame. She told me she was putting it by for a "rainy day" for when this music thing petered out.

ART BY @JOHN_CULSHAW86

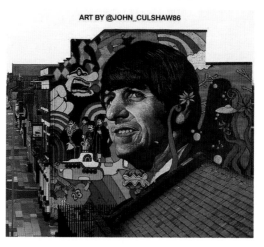

Scan this code with your smart-phone camera or QR Reader app to view the map, directions and more information.

The Grapes Pub

25 Mathew Street. Liverpool L2 6RE

Tel: +44 151-255-1525

The Grapes is a fun filled traditional Liverpool Pub. Established in 1960.

In those days the Cavern was an alcohol free venue and you could only be served with the soft drink of your choice. On many occasions the queue from the Cavern would stretch to the Grapes, no matter what weather conditions prevailed. Needless to say, the Grapes, being the only pub, was always crowded until closing time around 10 o'clock. The crowds were always huge on Mathew Street during any Beatles' performances and it was the overflow of the crowd that filled the Grapes.

There's memorabilia of the band dotted around including a photo strategically placed above the spot they used to sit. Go in the front door, bear right, go into the back dining room and the wooden "John Lennon" booth is the first one on the right. Sunday singalongs still abound, shared by locals and tourists alike.

Scan this code with your smart-phone camera or QR Reader app to view the map, directions and more information.

The Hard Day's Night Hotel

Central Buildings, North John Street, Liverpool L2 6RR

Tel: +44 151 236 1964

This beautifully appointed hotel pays homage to The Beatles in a big way. It is well worth a visit, even if only to see the photographs and tributes it pays to Liverpool's celebrated sons, and the memories the City has proudly retained.

It is in the City centre, a great tourist attraction, located close to the Cavern and many other Beatles' related locations.

I urge you to go online and see the magnificent layout of the rooms and suites, and the Beatle-themed bar and Blake's Restaurant, (named after artist Peter Blake) are well worth seeing…. Not to mention noshing in!

Freda Kelly celebrated her 70th Birthday in the beautiful John Lennon suite, complete with grand piano, and a magnificent array of floral tributes and other delights.

Truly a splendid venue for a celebration of her award-winning documentary film, Good Ol' Freda.

Scan the code with your smart-phone camera or QR Reader app to view the map, directions and more information.

The Jacaranda
21-23 Slater St, Liverpool L1 4BW
Tel: +44 151-708-2942

The Jacaranda is/was a popular haunt for young, hip people in the early days of The Mersey Sound, attracting both musicians and their fans to start off their evening before migrating to The Cavern for the real action. A particular favourite of John Lennon's, it was originally owned and operated by Allan Williams, The Beatles' first Manager, and has obviously undergone many changes over the past 60 years.

It has its own record store, Jacaranda Records, and is still a thriving, lively place to visit. Pay them a visit, you'll be glad you did. (Don't forget your ID).

Scan this code with your smart-phone camera or QR Reader app to view the map, directions and more information.

The Liverpool Beatles Museum

23 Mathew Street, Liverpool, L2 6RE

Tel: +44 151-236-1337

info@liverpoolbeatlesmuseum.com

The Liverpool Beatles Museum is housed in a large three storey former Victorian warehouse. It comprises over 300 primary and secondary source items of Beatles memorabilia that provide an invaluable resource for educators, and learners of all ages. Manager and Beatles historian Paul Parry, is a personal friend of former Beatles drummer Pete Best and of the museum's founder, Pete's brother Roag Best (son of Neil Aspinall and Mona Best).

Visitors will have the opportunity to explore first hand an unimaginable wealth of items, including original guitars and drums from the Hamburg days, John Lennon's itinerary from their first American tour, the white cello from Magical Mystery Tour, the medals John Lennon wore on the cover of Sgt Pepper, Paul McCartney's bass amp, George Harrison's ukulele as well as hundreds of other personal items, including never before seen letters, exclusive interviews with the band members and previously unseen footage of the Beatles.

Give my love to Roag and Pete if you see them!

Scan this code with your smart-phone camera or QR Reader app to view the map, directions and more information.

The Liverpool Institute
Mount St, Liverpool L1 9HF, United Kingdom
Tel: +44 151-330-3000

AKA Liverpool Institute High School for Boys ("The Inny")

The Liverpool Institute High School for Boys opened in 1825 and closed in 1985. During its time, it saw a lot of pupils who were destined for careers in the entertainment business.

These ranged from:

Neil Aspinall, originally The Beatles' Road Manager and later Managing Director of Apple Corp. Len Garry, one of the original members of The Quarrymen. Beatle George Harrison. Sir Paul McCartney, whose school records report that, having taken 0 and A levels, decided not to apply for Teacher's Training College, In July 1960 he left school to go off on the Beatles' first trip to Hamburg. But in 1995, he would return triumphantly to re-establish the property as The Liverpool Institute for the Performing Arts, (LIPA), which is still a thriving institution, serving the aspirations of young artistic people from all around the globe.

Paul's younger brother, Mike (McGear) McCartney also studied there from 1955 - 1961.

He then became famous as one of the members of the satirical group The Scaffold.

Liverpool Town Hall

High St, Liverpool L2 3SW

Tel: +44 151 233 3020

This majestic building stands in High Street at its junction with Dale Street, Castle Street, and Water Street in Liverpool. It is on the National Heritage List for England as a designated Grade I listed building, and described as "one of the finest surviving 18th-century town halls". The town hall was built between 1749 and 1754 and designed by John Wood the Elder, replacing an earlier town hall nearby.

On Friday, 10th July, 1964, this was the site for a Civic Reception held in The Beatles' honour following their triumphant return from America. Following the reception, they attended the premiere of their film *"A Hard Day's Night"* at The Odeon Cinema.

With Beatlemania at its height, the band were greeted by 200,000 fans as they made their way from the old Speke airport, while outside Liverpool Town Hall, another 20,000 fans gathered. They were given the freedom of the City by the Lord Mayor.

I was in the crowd that night, looking up at the Beatles, never dreaming for one moment that I was destined to become a part of their extended family a few months later. Scan to see the video from that night.

The White Star Pub
2-4 Rainford Gardens, Liverpool, L2 6PT UK
Tel:+44 151-231-6861

This friendly and welcoming little pub is just paces from The Cavern, and you can always be sure of a full house of music lovers, ranging from locals to tourists. In the back room aka "The Snug" is where Brian Epstein used to go and meet The Beatles after shows to settle the box office takings. There are lots of old photos adorning the walls.

This is also where Jim McCartney used to pop in once in a while - sometimes with Beatles Fan Club Secretary and Brian Epstein's Assistant, friend Freda Kelly on a market day (when the pubs were open all day), for a quick nip to get out of the cold at lunchtime.

They serve real ale, and it's always popular with all comers. It is a Victorian building that has stood the test of time, and never disappoints. They have put a roof on the Gents' toilet outside, but it still retains its original… shall we say "charm."

Sing songs tend to break out, and maybe even the occasional old codger playing the spoons. Its atmosphere is great, and you feel like you are at a family party - Liverpool style.

Check with them for current open hours. Covid-19 has created some limitations, although they are always anxious to please. It's a small place, filled with Beatles and Maritime memorabilia as The White Star Pub was named after The White Star Line, the famous shipping company that built The Titanic.

There are usually a few folkies in there who will burst into song at the drop of a hat.

Take your camera. You'll be sure to get some happy snaps of the crowd in there.

Scan this code with your smart-phone camera or QR Reader app to view the map, directions and more information.

Walton Hospital
Paul (and Ruth) McCartney's Birthplace
(Permanently closed)
Rice Lane, Prescot Street, Liverpool L9 1AE, United Kingdom

Mary McCartney gave birth to Paul in Paul & Michael (and Ruth) McCartney's on 18th June 1942, And his brother Michael on 7th January

1944. One of the many hospitals that she had worked at during her stint as a Midwife.

Walton Hospital had a long and incredible run. In fact, my own daughter, Ruth, was born there in February of 1960, and I always have fond memories of the kindness that I experienced there during pretty difficult times. (And that groovy Dr. Kirkland was pretty special too). All the Nurses and lots of the patients had the hots for him. He was like the George Clooney of his day.

It closed in 1964 when the entity was merged with Fazakerley Hospital as part of the National Health System.

The building still remains, silent and empty. Some have even said it's haunted.

But you might want to take a photograph of it while you're in the area.

Scan this code with your smart-phone camera or QR Reader app to view the map, directions and more information.

Ye Cracke Pub
13 Rice Street, Liverpool L1 9BB
Tel: +44 151-709-4171

The name is in "old English" with a "Y" at the beginning, and an "E" at the end. The final "E" is silent, thus it is pronounced The Crack. Despite its name, the pub opened in fact in the 19th Century. There is a small room known as "The War Room" in the oldest part of the pub, which is said to have been used for discussions on The Boer War. If you are a student of history, that war was between Britain and South Africa and ran between 16th December 1880 and March 23rd 1881.

There are about 20 prints of local scenes on the walls, all dating from the 1960's. John Lennon and his then girlfriend, Cynthia Powell used to go there when she and John were students at the Art School. And Stuart Sutcliffe and John would sit in the "snug" and down pints of Black Velvet at lunchtime. It has a quaint old-fashioned atmosphere, and is a warm welcoming spot. Ye Cracke was entwined with John Lennon's personal life, as he came here when he learned his mother, Julia, had been killed and he also brought Cynthia here after meeting her at a college dance.

Scan this code with your smart-phone camera or QR Reader app to view the map, directions and more information.

SECTION 3 :
LONDON TOWN

As the career trajectory of The Beatles began to emerge, Brian Epstein realised that they should all be living in London, where the action was, Television Studios, Recording Studios, and of course London airport, to speed them on their way to worldwide success.

What was Liverpool's loss was the world's gain. Liverpudlians always looked down their noses a bit at the Capital City, which always seemed to get all the attention. They called it "The Big Smoke." Until the Beatles became a worldwide phenomena, and then Liverpool was back in focus again, and remains so to this day.

And so it was that, in the Autumn of 1963, Brian found them a shared flat at 57 Green Street, which was OK for a little while, and by degrees, they each found permanent homes.

Brian always saw to it that they were properly looked after, and thanks to his trusty team of "handlers," they were always in the right place at the right time, properly fed, suitably dressed, and full of vim and vigour to amuse the press and their audiences.

I hope my chapters about London will prove interesting and give you some background of how their lives progressed.

To see all the destinations in this location, scan the code below with your Smartphone to load the McCartney.com page.

34 Montagu Square
London W1H

The square was named after Elizabeth Montagu, who was highly regarded by London society in the late 18th century. The basement flat in 34 Montagu Sq. was leased by Ringo for a short while in 1965, and after he moved out, he sublet the flat to friends, including Jimi Hendrix

But nowadays it is better known as the home of John Lennon and Yoko Ono who lived here in 1968. It was in October of that year that the police raided the flat and John and Yoko were charged with possession of cannabis.

Paul McCartney recorded some demo songs at that address, including "I'm Looking Through You", and also reportedly worked on various compositions, including "Eleanor Rigby". With the help of electronics technician and computer programmer Ian Sommerville, they converted the flat to a studio for Apple Corps' avant-garde Zapple label, eventually recording William S. Burroughs for spoken-word Zapple albums.

In addition, Jimi Hendrix and his manager, Chas Chandler, also later lived there with their girlfriends. Whilst living there, Hendrix evidently composed "The Wind Cries Mary."

For 3 months, John Lennon and Yoko Ono rented the flat, taking a photograph there that would become the cover of their *Two Virgins* album.

After the the Scotland Yard Police drug raid, the landlord of the property got an injunction against Ringo to prevent it from being used for anything illegal. Starr sold the lease in February 1969.

In 2010, this location aka John Lennon's London address was named as a Heritage Site and there was a blue marker plaque placed at the site.

Scan this code with your smart-phone camera or QR Reader app to view the map, directions and more information.

57 Green Street
Mayfair, London W1K 6RH, UK

This is a place that Beatles fans still like to include on their walking tours of the City, if only to pause to take a photograph.

57 Green Street in London's upscale Mayfair neighbourhood has the distinction of being the only home where all four Beatles lived at the same time – all crammed in together in "Flat L."

When The Beatles moved to London in the summer of 1963, they were staying at The President Hotel on Russell Square. It became apparent to Brian that as they were in London more than anywhere else, he needed to find them a suitable place to live.

That is how he came to decide on 57 Green Street. One can only imagine them all living in a shared apartment.

The sharing didn't last long for John and Cynthia, and they, together with baby Julian moved out as soon as they were able to find their own space.

Scan this code with your smart-phone camera or QR Reader app to view the map, directions and more information.

Abbey Road Studios
3 **Abbey Road** | St. John's **Wood London** NW8 9AY

Probably the world's most famous recording studios, where The Beatles created so much of their magic. See the code/link below for a complete list of all the superstars who worked there.

Although many other stars have recorded there, tourists are always hungry for information about their heroes, The Beatles.

Paul maintains a home close by, where he stays when in London. He used to sometimes take his Dad there in the late evenings when we were visiting, to sit in on their sessions. Jim always loved to recall these memories in the latter days of his life.

It was built in 1831 as a townhouse, and later, was converted to flats, and finally, in 1929 (the year I was born), The GramAphone (with an A) Company acquired it and thus the famous studios were born.

I always remember the lovely pots of hot tea that would mysteriously arrive on silver trolleys, with lots of caffeine to keep everyone going into the wee small hours.

Scan this code with your smart-phone camera or QR Reader app to view the map, directions and more information.

Apple Studios

3 Savile Row, Mayfair, London W1 3PB, UK

In 1968, following the untimely death of Brian Epstein in '67, The Beatles formed a new entity known as Apple Corps.

Its chief division was Apple Records. There were many other divisions, including Apple Films, Apple Publishing, Apple Retail, Apple Electronics etc. It was initially the brainchild of Paul McCartney, and the others grudgingly went along with the idea, until it came to fruition.

Their first premises was at 94 Baker Street, followed by a move to 95 Wigmore Street, and finally a move to 3 Savile Row, when they opened their Apple Boutique to much hoopla.

The plan was for Apple to eventually expand to a chain of premises throughout the country, to cater to the young and hip, and to encourage artistic folks to band together to make the world a happier place.

The building would eventually house a recording studio, where endless money was spent on kitting it out and filling it with luxury items, including whisky, other dubious substances, and many, many people sitting at desks, doing nobody-knows-what, having expensive lunches, hiring limos, etc. etc.

It was a veritable drain down which their money rapidly flowed.

It had a psychedelically decorated exterior, much to the chagrin of their neighbours, who consisted largely of bespoke tailors who catered to the rich and famous, even Royalty, and wealthy international clients.

Above the shop was a suite of offices, and always, outside on the street, were the faithful fans, who dubbed themselves "Apple Scruffs." They still communicate with one another to this day, via Facebook and other social media outlets.

On 30th January 1969, it became the location for the famous "Rooftop Concert" featuring "fifth Beatle" Billy Preston on keyboards as the band - as an entity - came together for the final time.

Scan this code with your smart-phone camera or QR Reader app to view the map, directions and more information.

The Bag O'Nails

Kingly Street, London W.1. UK

Public Transit: Oxford Circus, Piccadilly Circus

The Bag O'Nails was a hip place for musicians and their entourages to meet during the 1960's, and people who both performed and socialized included George Fame, Jimi Hendrix, Eric Burdon and many more.

It was a private members club, with a stringent doorman to make sure that only the "right" people gained access.

It closed in 1968 and re-opened as The Court. Its main claim to fame is that it is the place where Paul McCartney and Linda Eastman met for the first time on May 15th 1967.

Scan the code on the next page with your smart-phone camera or QR Reader app to view the map, directions and more information.

Buckingham Palace
Westminster, London SW1A 1AA
Tel: +44 303 123 7300

Buckingham Palace surely does not need any introduction, this central focal point of London's sightseeing tours, and Royals watchers.

It is listed here because it is where The Beatles were bestowed with their MBE's which really secured their place in British History. The Ceremony took place in October 1965.

Two years later, they wore their medals on the album cover of Sgt. Pepper's Lonely Hearts Club Band. Four years later John decided he no longer wanted to keep his.

HM Queen Elizabeth II bestowed the Honors, while the world's news media watched. TV viewing figures of the event were at an all time high. I remember Paul's Dad nearly bursting with pride, to think that his son had achieved such recognition.

John was later to return his in protest of the Vietnam War and various matters that angered him at the time. He had given the actual Award to his Aunt Mimi who proudly displayed it in her Poole, Dorset home, which John had kindly provided for her. He sent his Chauffeur to ask if he could borrow it, and she had no idea what was afoot. It was something that caused her great sadness.

Limited tours of the Palace are sometimes available, and anyone interested should Google the Buckingham Palace website for current information.

Scan this code with your smart-phone camera or QR Reader app to view the map, directions and more information.

Caxton Hall
Site of Ringo and Maureen's 1965 Wedding
10 Caxton Street St. James Park, London, UK

Caxton Hall has seen many celebrity weddings over the years. They include Elizabeth Taylor, Diana Dors, Peter Sellers, Orson Welles, Joan Collins, Barry Gibb, Adam Faith, Billy Butlin and Roger Moore. (But not to each other)!

Even earlier in history, Prime Minister Anthony Eden married Clarissa Spencer-Churchill, the niece of Sir Winston.

It was also the venue where the Suffragettes would meet to plan their strategy to obtain the rights of women to vote.

And on 11th February 1965, Ringo Starr and Mo (Maureen) Cox were married, accompanied by Brian Epstein, Elsie and Harry Graves, (Ringo's parents), Mo's parents, and George and John. Paul was away on holiday in Tunisia.

There have been many other notable happenings. Sir Winston Churchill made his wartime speeches from there, and Patti Boyd first attended a lecture about Transcendental Meditation, which information she conveyed to George and his buddies, and so their whole relationship with The Maharishi Mahesh Yogi began.

And episodes of Downton Abbey were also shot there.

Scan this code with your smart-phone camera or QR Reader app to view the map, directions and more information.

Decca Studios

NOW CLOSED

165 Broadhurst Gardens, West Hampstead, London, UK

The Beatles relationship with Decca Records goes back to the time when Brian Epstein had been diligently pursuing them re obtaining a recording contract with one of the majors.

Decca's A & R man, Mike Smith had travelled to Liverpool to see the boys at The Cavern, and was sufficiently impressed to invite them down to London to audition on 1st January 1962.

So on 31st December, 1961, Neil Aspinall drove them to London, but he lost his way, and the trip took ten hours. They arrived after 10:00 p.m. New Year's Eve, *"just in time to see the drunks jumping into Trafalgar Square fountain"* as John put it.

Paul, John, George and Pete Best arrived at Decca Studios at 10 a.m. on New Year's Day, not the best day to embark on such a venture. As it turned out, Mike Smith had partied a little too hard the night before, and arrived, very hung over, as well as suffering from a recent car crash, so the proceeding session started later than planned.

In those days, it was customary for the "victims" to play between two and five songs, but as it turned out, they wound up playing 15 numbers, and they broke for lunch and resumed in the afternoon. You can imagine how tired they must have been at this stage.

It was about a month before they learned that Decca had rejected them. The general opinion was that *"guitar groups were on their way out"* and someone even said *"The Beatles are on their way out."* Oops!

However, undaunted, Brian continued his pursuit, and approached EMI and was put in touch with Norrie Paramor, Walter Ridley and Normal Newell, but all three of them declined the offer.

They eventually signed with an EMI subsidiary, Parlophone, after Producer George Martin heard the recorded session they had done at Decca, and was interested to meet them.

Incidentally, that original tape from Decca, was later sold at auction to a Japanese collector for $35,000, so maybe it wasn't that bad after all?

The London Palladium
8 Argyll St, Soho, London W1F 7TF, United Kingdom
Tel: +44 207 492 0834

This famed theatre has been the scene of many great performances, including a Beatles' Royal Variety Command Performance, at least one of which was distinguished by John Lennon's remark asking the rich patrons to "*rattle yer jewellery*." Whereas, the peasants were merely asked to applaud.

The London Palladium is, without doubt, London's most famous theatre, and to get to stand on that stage is one tremendous buzz, according to the boys, and several musicians who have been privileged to play there.

Living in England at the time, Sunday Night at The London Palladium was the biggest TV event of the week, and the pubs did precious little business until after the show was over. Then the husbands, (and maybe the wives) would spill out for a couple of adult beverages.

So what a thrill it was then, to see our local heroes on that stage. Never mind yer Ed Sullivan, this was the apex for me.

Scan this code with your smart-phone camera or QR Reader app to view the map, directions and more information.

Marylebone Town Hall Register Office

97-113 Marylebone Rd, Marylebone, London NW1 5PT
Tel: +44 (0)20 7641 7500

The building dates back in part to the 18th century. The old courthouse became the headquarters of the Metropolitan Borough of Marylebone in 1900.

Throughout the years, it has undergone many changes, most of which were Municipal and City oriented, relating to the running of the borough, until finally, it is now mostly used for the solemnization of marriages.

Cilla Black and Bobby Willis were married there in January 1969. Paul and Linda tied the knot in March 1969. Fellow Beatle, Ringo Starr and Barbara Bach were married in April 1981.

It has been a long time favourite location for weddings of people of many backgrounds, including Liam Gallagher and Nicole Appleton who were wed in February 2008. Also Sean Bean and Georgina Sutcliffe, also in February 2008, and more recently, Sir Paul McCartney and Nancy Shevell in October 2011.

Indeed, a popular spot for celebrity nuptials. And no doubt a regular spot on the dial for many Paparazzi.

London Marylebone Railway Station

Great Central House Melcombe Place, London NW1 6JJ

Tel: +44 345 600 5165

Marylebone has seen many expansions over the years, and came to global fame when The Beatles shot scenes for *A Hard Day's Night,* accompanied by the screams of hundreds of girls, and even a few boys, when they realized that their heroes were in town.

That was in March of 1964, and since that time, the location has seen many more visitors than ever, cameras in hand. Director Richard Lester had more to deal with than he had anticipated.

And it was during that filming that George Harrison first met Patti Boyd, who would become his wife. But that's another story…

George later shot his solo scene at Twickenham Studios. His line was: "Oh, I'm not wearing that, it's grotty." (As in grotesque). It was a made up word by Alun Owen, the screenwriter.

Other movies have also been shot there, including The Ipcress File and The Day of the Triffids.

Scan this code with your smart-phone camera or QR Reader app to view the map, directions and more information.

The Royal Albert Hall
Kensington Gore, London SW7 2AP
Tel: +44 20-7589-821

No Brit worth his or her salt can ever admit that they have never been thrilled by the Last Night of The Proms, the yearly festival of music initiated by Sir Henry Wood. They were dubbed "Promenade Concerts" as the vast majority of the audience stood in the arena, whilst the more well-heeled visitors sat in boxes on real chairs.

I had the pleasure of being there once only in my lifetime, along with my first husband, Eddie Williams, when we queued up for hours to get in to the cheapest area of the arena, (standing room only), and be a part of this magnificent spectacle, with the orchestra conducted by Sir Thomas Beecham, culminating in the singing of *Jerusalem* and *Land of Hope And Glory*, when we all waved our Union flags and sang our little lungs out.

I never hear it without being transported back to that very moment. It grieves me to learn that in 2020 it is being considered to remove the vocals from future performances, and just play the music to a silent audience, as it is considered as being offensive to some of the non-British people who have been fortunate enough to have made a home in England.

The Beatles made their first appearance there on April 18 1963, as part of a BBC taping of a show called The BBC Show *Swinging Sound '63*, featuring other acts including Kenny Lynch, Del Shannon and others. There was a story about them being asked to "play quietly" which John Lennon strongly objected to, and when he began arguing with the production people, someone quietly reminded him that this WAS the BBC and if you ruffled their feathers, they may not play your records, so presumably he calmed down.

Jane Asher was there that night, on an assignment for The Radio Times, and posed for photos with the Beatles, every bit the Beatle fan.

Their second appearance was on 15th September 1963 at a show promoted by the Printing Trade, and this time they shared the bill with The Rolling Stones.

Yoko and John performed there too, when Yoko recorded "AOS" on stage, accompanied by John Lennon on guitar, and the couple appeared on stage in a white bag to promote their 'bagism' period during a huge Christmas event staged by many of the alternative scene.

The Royal Albert Hall has certainly seen a cornucopia of art forms over the years. In the beginning, it cost one shilling to promenade.

The last time I checked, it was 5 quid, and still worth every penny. Truly, an inspiring occasion. I still remember it with strong emotions.

The Saville Theatre

135 Shaftesbury Avenue, Covent Garden, London

Tel: +44 333-014-4501

Now known as The Odeon, Covent Garden

Since its days as a theatre, it has now become a four screen movie theatre. Brian Epstein, himself a former drama student, leased the theatre in 1965 and presented both plays and rock and roll music shows.

The venue became notorious for its Sunday night concerts. During a performance by Chuck Berry, members of the audience stormed the stage and the police were brought in to subdue them and empty the theatre.

Jimi Hendrix appeared there, and also such people as The Move, Procul Harum, Nirvana, Cream, Fairport convention, The Incredible String Band and The Bee Gees.

The Beatles took over the Saville stage for the making of their music video *"Hello, Goodbye"* and Yoko Ono also used the Theatre to perform her *"The Fog Machine: Music of the Mind."* which also included her *Bottoms, (Film No. 4)* in the men's room during the concert.

The Rolling Stones also held two shows on December 21st 1969. Georgie Fame and The Blue Flames were also a popular recurring act.

Scan this code with your smart-phone camera or QR Reader app to view the map, directions and more information.

SECTION 4 : LOS ANGELES

Los Angeles has always been a favourite of The Beatles, owning property and working in studios around the area.

L.A. people professing to be pretty "laid back" do seem to have given them more space, generally speaking, although not in the days when they were still a working band.

As time progresses, however, folks have become more accustomed to celebrities, and moving in similar circles, visiting stadiums (or should I say "stadia?"), and coming across them in public places, restaurants etc.

But the good old Paparazzi never miss an opportunity, because an exclusive photo can earn them big bucks. I guess that will never change.

A very popular tourist spot is The Capitol Records building, outside of which is where their Stars on The Walk of Fame can be seen.

The Hollywood Bowl and The Hollywood sign are high on the list too. I will confess that when I first came to live here, over 30 years ago, I was as big a tourist as anyone, and I value the memories I have of many happy times spent in the pursuit of the glamour of Hollywood.

Now, as an elderly (but thankfully, still hard working) old broad in her 90's, I am content to see it from afar, via the many forms of entertainment that are available to us electronically.

I hope my readers find something to suit their LA tastes in the following pages' destinations.

1567 Blue Jay Way
Hollywood Hills, Los Angeles

Blue Jay Way was an address where George Harrison stayed on one of his sojourns to Los Angeles in August 1967. The house belonged to Peggy Lee's manager.

He flew into LAX from London, jetlagged, and waited for Derek Taylor, The Beatles' Publicist to arrive with some paperwork he needed to sign, but Derek was delayed, so George passed the time by writing a song, which he called "Blue Jay Way" and it made its way on to the Magical Mystery Tour album.

It was a very foggy night, and Derek got lost in the Canyons of the Hollywood Hills, leaving George to fend for himself for an unexpectedly long time. The composition was in psychedelic mode, as were the minds of The Beatles at that time in their lives.

It was just before George went to Haight-Ashbury, San Francisco, where Flower Power was all the rage.

Scan this code with your smart-phone camera or QR Reader app to view the map, directions and more information.

2850 Benedict Canyon
Beverly Hills, CA, 90210 USA

Thanks to MeetTheBeatlesforReal.com for the image. Scan the code at the end of this location to visit their website and in-depth article on this subject including an interview with the former, late great Chauffeur Alf Bicknell.

This is a house that The Beatles rented from Zsa Zsa Gabor. It was up in the Hollywood Hills, and they hoped it would prove to be a peaceful getaway. They planned to relax and spend time in the pool.

It was just up the side from the Beverly Hills Hotel, in a canyon. There were several bedrooms, and the boys and crew were taken care of by a young man from a local catering company.

Every day, he, along with one or two female assistants took care of the food, laying the tables, providing the sumptuous meals and drinks, and clearing away as if by magic at the end of the day. Next day, they would reappear and repeat the process.

But it wasn't long before one of the local radio DJs spilled the beans, and from then on, they were besieged by ardent fans.

It was in August of 1965, from August 23rd to 27th, when they had a few days off to recharge their batteries ready for the next stint.

Alf Bicknell, their driver, did his best to keep the fans at bay, but not always with success. He said in one of his interviews that he thought a girl had dropped into the pool from a helicopter. At least, that was his recollection of it. Or maybe she had just sneaked in over the wall. But who knows. Some of those fans were very inventive.

Scan the code on the next page with your smart-phone camera or QR Reader app to view the map, directions and more information.

Capitol Records
1750 Vine Street, Los Angeles, CA

The blinking light atop the tower spells out the word "Hollywood" in Morse code. It is classified as a cultural monument.

The recording facility has eight echo chambers, which were engineered by Les Paul and also main studios A, B and C.

Frank Sinatra had close ties to the studios and recorded much of his work there. He was particularly fond of the Neumann U47 mic, which he always carried around with him and used for sessions. His original mic and stool are still available to artists who rent the studios. Frank's first album recorded at Capitol was *Frank Sinatra Conducts, Tone Poems of Color.*

Then in 2012, Studio A received a new AMS Neve 88R mixing console, designed and built for uber engineer Al Schmitt and Paul McCartney.

The Beatles - as a group - never actually cut records there, but the label offices were in the tower so over the years they spent a good amount of time in the building. It was a favourite of The Beach Boys, and many other famous artists.

Always a good photo op, and the four Beatles' Stars on the Hollywood Walk of Fame are outside of the building too. I am lucky to have been in on various sessions there over the years...

Then in November of 2018 we were honoured to be a part of legendary Beatles' Engineer Geoff Emerick's private memorial hosted in Studio A and special thanks to Paula Salvatore.

Dodger Stadium

Elysian Park Avenue, Los Angeles

The Beatles appeared at Dodger Stadium on August 28th 1966, the night before they played their last show at Candlestick Park.

It was another venture funded by Bob Eubanks, in addition to the twice that they had played The Hollywood Bowl.

They only played about a 30-minute set, and there were four supporting acts, to ensure that the audience got their money's worth. Although, tickets were only in the range of some $3.50 to about $6.00. The cheapest seats were reserved for the military.

The Beatles only performed 11 songs. And by this time, the boys were getting pretty jaded at not being able to hear themselves due to the screaming crowds. They felt that the end was near and that they would rather be in the studios recording albums, which they ultimately returned to.

The number of security was not at all big enough, 102 security guards to be precise. Dozens of people were hurt, and 25 were arrested and hauled away to cool off. There was a rush for the main gates as their set was coming to a close. Their limo was forced to turn back and take the boys to an underground dugout, where they were locked in for a couple of hours for their own safety.

The crowd became violent, hurling bottles and wooden barricades. Many of the crowd were still in the Stadium long after the Beatles had exited.

Tony Barrow, their Press Officer gave a statement:

"They had arrived there in an armoured car and at the end, when we were ready to pull away, thousands had stormed the grounds and exits and the driver yelled to us to hang on tightly. He slammed the vehicle into reverse and raced us to an underground team dugout, where we stayed for a good couple of hours until the panic had died down.

We later tried with three decoy limos, but that didn't work either. The crazed fans caused so much damage that one of the cars was completely destroyed. We eventually got away in an Ambulance that crashed into a heap of broken fencing. Extra squads of Police from the Sheriff's Department eventually got us out in an armoured car."

The group finally got to their rented house at 7665 Carson Road, Beverly Hills, before flying to San Francisco the next afternoon for their final gig at Candlestick Park.

The Hard Rock Cafe

6801 Hollywood Blvd Ste 105, Los Angeles, CA 90028

Tel: +323 464-7625

This is another place where you can see lots of Beatles and other celebrity artifacts and photos, a great opportunity for the Day Tripper to not only see, but hear great music and even grab a beer and a burger, (or whatever is your choice). Good varied menu.

This is one really busy tourist spot, so you may have to wait for a table. But in the meantime, you can meander around, even use the loo, if you need to, until your table is ready for you to have a good tuck in. Another great photo op.

Scan this code with your smart-phone camera or QR Reader app to view the map, directions and more information.

The Hollywood Bowl

2301 N. Highland Avenue, Los Angeles, CA 90035
Tel: 323-850-2000

This Hollywood iconic amphitheater in the Hollywood Hills has been in the forefront of Los Angeles Tourism since it opened in 1922.

It is considered one of the best music venues in America and is run by the Hollywood Philharmonic Association. It has a capacity of 1,700.

Many of you will be familiar with the album: *The Beatles Live at The Hollywood Bowl.* This was released in May 1977 and includes many of the songs that they performed on their stints in August of 1964 and 1965. It is released on Capitol Records in America and Canada, and Parlophone in the UK.

Former DJ, Bob Eubanks featured largely in their being booked at The Hollywood Bowl. Brian Epstein knew it was a very prestigious gig, and badly wanted it for them. The fee requested was a whopping $25,000 for one night, a huge amount of money in those days.

Bob and his business partner owned a house together as an investment, so they took the plunge and mortgaged that property to raise a Bank Loan to fund the show, and it finally came together.

In 1964, there was no internet, thus no online ticket reservation system and tickets could only be bought at the box office, Automobile Club offices or Wallich's Music City stores. And in 1965 there was only one way to pay, by mail. Yes, in an envelope, with a postage stamp. Remember them?

Although forced to cancel its 2020 season due to the Pandemic, it stayed high on the list of places to see for tourists, and in particular, Beatles fans who want to visit and take pictures.

The acoustics are magical, even if you are up in the "nosebleed" section, way up high in the cheaper seats. I have enjoyed many a wonderful evening under the stars up there, as well as in the front of house, where they have boxes to be enjoyed, bringing your picnic baskets and wine of your choice. Various catering policies and regulations tend to change according to the type of show, so it's always best to check in advance to learn about all the options.

In some cases, you are encouraged to place your food and drink orders for the boxes by 4 p.m. on the day before the show.

Always allow yourself plenty of time to get there and park, as traffic slows to a crawl once you get in the vicinity, and believe me, there is plenty of it, including buses, which clog the lanes. The City also provides a lot of park and ride facilities, where you can leave your car, journey to the Bowl in a comfortable air conditioned bus, and not have to be concerned about your arrival time.

There are also shuttle areas close to the venue. You can buy your tickets along with your entrance tickets to the Bowl. There are often Senior's $10 rush tickets for select Tuesdays and Thursdays, so you should call them in advance to find out availability.

The Whisky-a-GoGo

8901 W Sunset Blvd, West Hollywood, CA 90069
Tel: (310) 652-4202

It is the place where The Beatles met with Jayne Mansfield. At a press conference when they landed on 8/23/64, Paul had expressed a wish to meet her, and one of their "peeps" set it up, not, as they would have preferred, in a more intimate setting, but in a booth in the noisy club. But it all went well, and they took some great photos.

Previously, it was always listed as a 24-hour joint, with good food, great music, the flowing booze of your choice, including, of course. Whisky. Oh, and be sure to have your ID to prove your age if you want to drink alcohol.

This applies to all drinking establishments in America. The legal age is 21 in all States. It's always best to check with your tour people or hotel Concierge.

Since the 60's, The Whisky has been a massive tourist attraction.

Crowds outside day and night, and if you are looking for a lively night (or early morning), this has always been the place. Call them to check on their current opening hours.

It's a once in a lifetime experience, but earplugs are always a good idea. If it's full, go across to the street to The Viper Room for a while.

SECTION 5 : NEW YORK

The Beatles' times in New York, both as a group and individually, came later in their career, by which time, they had all experienced so much worldwide. Their true launch into worldwide fame was, of course, their first appearance on the Ed Sullivan Show, and from then on, nothing was the same.

Although they had been experiencing a great deal of success and adulation at home in the UK, it was nothing compared to how their lives would be from the day they landed at JFK and began to conquer America.

Their privacy was no more, and wherever they went, they needed not only their trusty Neil and Mal, but Security Guards, and sometimes US Police and even Fire Marshals.

With the growth of their fame, came a disturbing aspect of the violence that could sometimes erupt, and it pained them greatly to see what could happen at venues where the fans tried to rush the stage, or rock their vehicles as they were leaving the venue at the end of a performance. And sadly, it would become the last City in which John Lennon would live.

But to this day, the fans only remember the happy times, which is really how it should be, and Social Media has helped many of them to cement new friendships, which are a great comfort to Beatles Fans around the world.

And then there's the Fests for Beatles Fans, run by Mark and Carol Lapidos and family out of New York. Since the outbreak of the Pandemic in 2020 they have moved from their usual face-to-face family-type gatherings, by now moving online to virtual ones, the reach has become even bigger, as people can watch the activities from the comfort of their homes through the wonders of technology. Who can complain about that? Start spreadin' the news…

105 Bank Street
Greenwich Village, New York NY 10014
A temporary home for John and Yoko

PLEASE DO NOT DISTURB THE RESIDENTS

After their stay at The St. Regis Hotel, John and Yoko moved to a more intimate apartment on Bank Street in the artsy Greenwich Village. They liked its quaintness, and they had more privacy than being "on show" in a big hotel.

Unfortunately, they had a robbery at the property, after which they didn't feel quite so safe, and it led them in turn to move to their apartment in The Dakota Building, where Yoko still maintains a residence.

A nice photo op for your memory book, but don't forget, it is private property, so please be conscious of the need for privacy of the residents.

Scan this code with your smart-phone camera or QR Reader app to view the map, directions and more information.

Carnegie Hall

881 7th Avenue, between West 56th and West 57th Streets, New York, NY USA

Tel: 1-212-247-7800

The magnificent Concert Hall consists of three separate auditoriums. The Stern Auditorium, The Perelman Stage, and the Weill Recital Hall. It has a total seating capacity of 3,671.

It has played host to an array of presentations, ranging from operatic, to orchestral to modern day popular entertainment of many stripes.

NEW YORK. MERSEYSIDE IN CARNEGIE HALL: THE FOUR BEATLES DURING THEIR FEBRUARY 12 CONCERT IN ONE OF NEW YORK'S FAMOUS MUSICAL CENTRES. The Beatles arrived by air in New York on Feb. 7 to a tumultuous welcome from some 5000 teenagers for a ten-day tour of the United States; and continued in their usual conquering and disarming way, parrying critical remarks with their own especial engaging humour.

The Management were originally not prepared to book Rock'n'Roll acts, but made an exception when Bill Hailey appeared at a benefit in 1955.

Then along came Sid Bernstein, who convinced the officials that allowing the Beatles to perform there would further international understanding between the United States and Great Britain, and he won them over. The Beatles played 2 shows there during their first trip to the United States on February 12, 1964. Having just returned from their appearance at Washington, DC's Coliseum, the Beatles sold out both shows, with a band called The Briarwoods opening for them. Producer George Martin had planned to record the concerts for a future live album, although he was denied permission, despite Capitol Records' efforts, by the American Federation of Musicians. Much to John Lennon's annoyance, there were LOTS of VIPs seated ON THE STAGE during the performance - New York Society made sure their children literally had a front row seat.

After that, it was game on for the rockers to get on board, and since then, they have been a staple of the shows. They also relented and allowed blues, country, and jazz artists to join their roster. Rumor is that a pedestrian on Fifty-seventh Street, Manhattan, stopped Jascha Heifetz and inquired, "Could you tell me how to get to Carnegie Hall?" "Yes," said Heifetz. "Practice!"

This has also been attributed to others, such as Jack Benny over the years.

JFK Airport New York

JFK Access Road, One Idlewild Drive, NY 11430

Tel: 1 212-806-9000

JFK is located in Queens, New York, 16 miles southeast of Midtown Manhattan. Nowadays there is a fantastic recreation of the original TWA Terminal, where the Beatles landed, in the form of a hotel. They have 4 suites named for each Beatle.

The airport features 5 terminals and 4 runways. It opened in 1948 and was known as Idlewild Airport. Following John F. Kennedy's assassination it was re-named JFK Airport in his honour.

There is a commemorative plaque at the site where The Beatles received a tumultuous welcome when their plane landed there on 7th February 1964. They had never experienced anything quite like it in their lives. But they would soon become accustomed to that kind of hysteria. No wonder it began to be known as *Beatlemania*.

Along with the multitudes of journalists, photographers and film crews, there was a massive Police presence to make sure that they remained safe until they reached their hotel, where they became actual prisoners in their own suite. They couldn't even sleep at night, as the shrill screams of the fans outside continued around the clock.

I can only imagine what it must have been like for the Hotel staff on the front desk. Their security staff were kept fully occupied making sure that none of the girls managed to sneak in, either through the regular entrance, or via the delivery bays around the back of the building.

Scan this code with your smart-phone camera or QR Reader app to view the map, directions and more information.

Smith's Bar
701 8th Avenue, W. 44th Street, NY, 10036
Tel: 1-212-246-3268

This snazzy little bar was close to The Hit Factory, where John Lennon loved to work. Rumour has it that he would frequently pop in there for a feed between sessions, and the locals would say he was really friendly and eager to tell them what he was up to, musically. It is still a thriving little place, frequented by both locals and tourists.

You can often find one of the regulars ready to re-tell tales of the days when John was one of their fellow customers.

Pop in. You'll be glad you did.

Scan this code with your smart-phone camera or QR Reader app to view the map, directions and more information.

Strawberry Fields

Central Park West, New York

(between 71st and 74th Streets)

Tel: 1 212-639-9675

Nearest Subway 72nd Street Station

Strawberry Fields is a 2.5-acre landscaped section in New York City's Central Park, designed by the landscape architect Bruce Kelly, that is dedicated to the memory of John Lennon who died in 1980.

It was officially dedicated on October 9th, 1984 - John's birthday. Yoko worked with the landscape artist, Bruce Kelly, and New York Central Park Conservancy to create this beautiful memorial to the memory of John Lennon who was dedicated to world peace. When the trees are bare, the garden is visible from the high floors of The Dakota Building, where Yoko still resides.

It is a mecca for tourists, who daily lay flowers on the beautiful mosaic. The surroundings are peaceful, as would befit such an iconic place of reflection. Groups often join hands and sing "*Imagine*," which is very moving.

Scan this code with your smart-phone camera or QR Reader app to view the map, directions and more information.

The Dakota Building
21 West 72nd Street, New York, NY 10023, USA

PLEASE DO NOT DISTURB THE RESIDENTS

The Dakota was built in 1884 and designed by architect Henry J. Hardenbergh, who also designed the Plaza Hotel. The building offers legendary New York City living thanks to its incredible architecture, spectacular Central Park Views, and illustrious list of current and past residents. New York City's Dakota is probably the City's most famous residence, where many celebrities and social elite have lived. The famed home of John Lennon and Yoko Ono, where he was shot and killed by Mark Chapman as he was autographing an album for him on December 8th, 1980.

Although a private building, it's a tourist mecca for worldwide fans of John Lennon.

Yoko continues to maintain a property and live there.

Trivia:

The original owner's former apartment has sterling-silver floors.

Singer Sewing Machine Company founder Edward Clark commissioned The Dakota as a $1 million apartment building for 60 families, including his own. Clark, however, died in 1882, two years before the building was completed.

It has been a magnet for the rich and famous since it opened way back in the year 1884.

The building was reportedly fully rented before it even opened, thanks to a glowing New York Times review. The Steinway family, of Steinway piano fame, was one of The Dakota's first residents. Though he died in 1883, Peter Tchaikovsky is said to have lived there (perhaps he lived in it before its completion).

Actress Lauren Bacall owned a nine-room apartment for 53 years that recently sold for $23.5 million. Other notable residents have included author Harlan Coben, U2's Bono, Rex Reed, Jack Palance, Lillian Gish, Boris Karloff, Rosemary Clooney, Connie Chung, and Maury Povich.

Even Celebrities don't get special treatment

Notable celebrities who have been rejected by The Dakota co-op board include Melanie Griffith and Antonio Banderas, Cher, Billy Joel, Madonna, Carly Simon, Alex Rodriguez, Judd Apatow, and Tea Leoni.

Rumours

It's rumored that $30,000 is buried under the floor of Lennon and Ono's apartment. According to author Stephen Birmingham's 1996 book, "Life at the Dakota," the previous resident of John and Yoko's apartment hid the money under the master-bedroom floor.

Whether that's true will remain a question, as the board refuses to destroy the floor to solve the mystery.

The Ed Sullivan Theatre

1697/99 Broadway

Between W. 53rd and 54th Streets, Manhattan, New York 10002

Tel: 1-212-975-3700

This iconic, intimate theatre first opened in 1927, and has been closed and re-opened twice since then.

Over the years, it has been home to such shows as The Merv Griffin Show, The Rosie O'Donnell Show, Late Night With David Letterman, and more recently, The Late Show with Stephen Colbert.

It is on the ground floor of a multi storey office building, and was, in recent years, converted to a television studio.

The Beatles made their historic first of two appearances there on 9th February 1964, when their world opened up, and their vista became oh so much bigger than their small hometown of Liverpool. Despite all its other claims to fame, it will forever be known as the place where The Beatles launched their worldwide career.

It is on the National Register of Historic Buildings, and its interior classed as a landmark by the NYC Preservation Commission.

Scan this code with your smart-phone camera or QR Reader app to view the map, directions and more information.

The Hit Factory
Now SearSound
353 West 48th Street, 6th Floor NY, NY 10036
Tel: 212-582-5380
Nearest Subway 50th Street

Situated on 48th Street and Ninth Avenue, this is where Yoko and John collaborated on their album, *Double Fantasy*. Sear Sound moved to the location in 1991, and Ono continued to use the studio to track and mix her projects.

The 2 businesses have no affiliation, however there is some Beatles memorabilia in the studio. There are still some tape machines that were used by the Beatles at Abbey Road which they purchased some years ago and modified.

ABOUT THE AUTHOR

Photo courtesy Barbara Burton, London, June 1967.

Ruth, Angie, Jim & Paul in St. John's Wood

Angela Lucia McCartney was born in Liverpool UK in November of 1929. She married her first husband Eddie in 1956, and daughter Ruth was born in February 1960. Sadly, Angie was widowed in ‹62, and then in '64, her old friends Mike and Bette introduced her to their Uncle Jim McCartney.

They married that November and spent 12 loving years together, with Angie and Ruth at his side when he passed over to the great tea dance in the sky in March of 1976. Angie has lived through WW2, widowhood (twice), the 2020 Pandemic and many crazy times in the past, including celebrating the announcements of #1 chart hits with friend and frequent house-guest John Lennon over breakfast (and tea) at Rembrandt, the Liverpool home in the 60's.

Today, she's as feisty as ever and runs an online organic tea company, **Mrs. McCartney's Teas and** a fruit wine / cocktail mixer company **Mrs. McCartney's Wines.** This is her third book following 2013's **My Long and Winding Road** and 2019's **Your Mother Should Know.**

FIND ANGIE ONLINE

Every Tuesday, she hosts an online Facebook Live chat show entitled **Teaflix Tuesdays** with daughter Ruth which you can find on her page at 11:30am SHARP Los Angeles / Pacific time @drangiemccartney

A percentage of the profits of all of Angie's ventures are donated to The Linda McCartney Breast Cancer Centre in her hometown.

Angie thrives on tea, humour, positive thinking and of course, wine!

Visit her online at :

www.mrsmccartneysteas.com

and

www.mrsmccartneyswines.com

NOTES, PEOPLE I MET AND THINGS I'D LIKE TO REMEMBER:

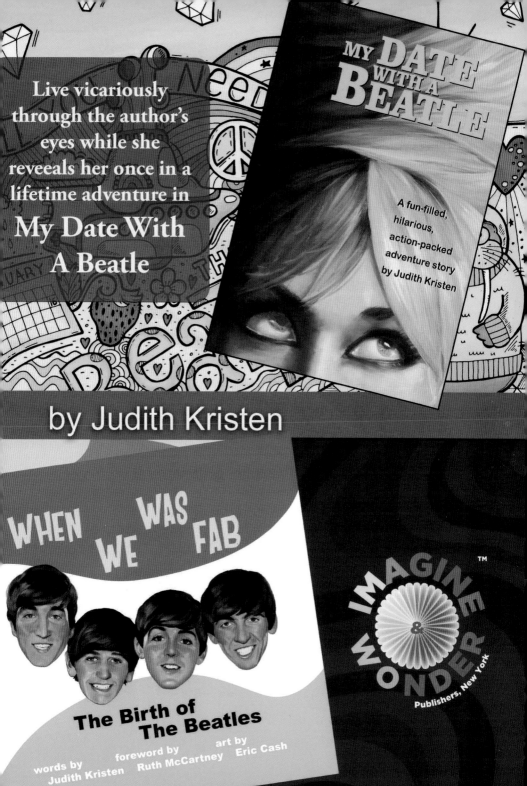

Live vicariously through the author's eyes while she reveeals her once in a lifetime adventure in **My Date With A Beatle**

MY DATE WITH A BEATLE

A fun-filled, hilarious, action-packed adventure story by Judith Kristen

by Judith Kristen

WHEN WE WAS FAB

The Birth of The Beatles

words by
Judith Kristen

foreword by
Ruth McCartney

art by
Eric Cash

IMAGINE & WONDER™
Publishers, New York

Also available from this author at www.Imagineandwonder.com

Scan the QR code to find other
amazing adventures and more from
www.ImagineAndWonder.com

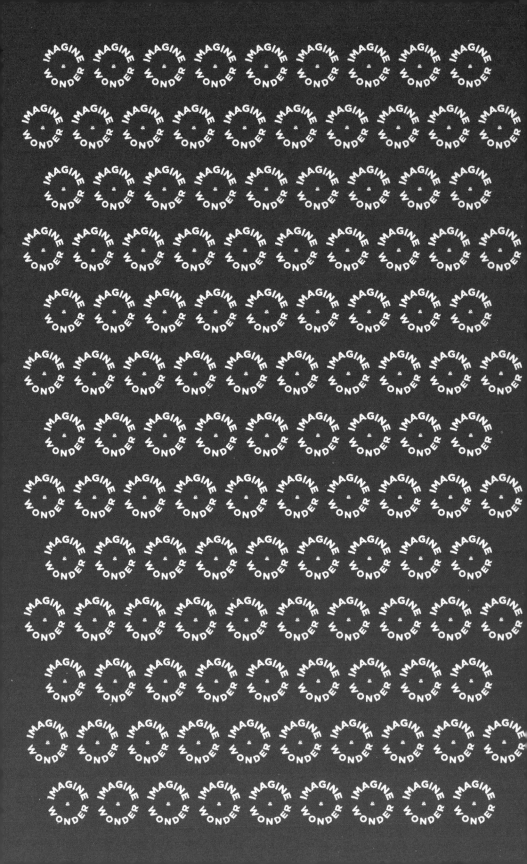